Glory Girl

Stella Gipson Polk

EAKIN PRESS
Austin, Texas

*For my granddaughter Patricia
whose personality I have
borrowed for Eve.*

Stella Gipson Polk

INTRODUCTION

When you read my sister's story, you go into a world of quiet broken only when John Devvies gives his Rebel Yell. You sense Granny Hutch's daily need to wrest a living from a remote Texas farm. You go with her and Eve to thump watermelons ripening on a hillslope; you pick blackberries growing wild along Dog Branch, and you follow step by step the process of making molasses.

You witness ecology at its grass roots—the giving of nature to man and the reverse giving of man to nature.

Stella has written with a sensitivity which reveals her knowledge of rural life. As children, she and I grew up in that natural setting. Both of us still share a deep love for the Texas Hill Country.

Of her book, Stella says, "If for the space of an hour I have caused one reader to forget city walls and pushing crowds and go into Eve's world of hills and horizons, then I am content."

Fred Gipson
Mason, Texas

1

Eve hid in the hollyhocks and waited. This had to be Granny Hutch's cabin.

"Take the pasture road east," freighter Millican had told her. "You'll get to a little bitty shack looking south. It's got a low shed room on behind, sorter like a dog squatting on its haunches. That'll be where Granny Hutch lives."

Now Eve stared out from the hollyhocks at the weather-beaten cabin. The chimney on the west wall had its broad back to her. The window by it glared at her through the limbs of a tall postoak. Around the cabin, everywhere she looked, hills closed her in. Pasture land stretched silently toward hills which marked the horizon.

Suddenly Eve was afraid, more afraid than she'd ever been in her whole life. Why hadn't she ridden the truck to Marty with freighter Millican?

"I won't be afraid," she whispered fiercely. "I'll make a rhyme. Rhymes always make the 'fraid go away." She struck her fist in her left palm and chanted:

"I'm a runaway orphan from Home of the Tyne.

I'm twelve years old. It's June, 1969."

A woman came out on the stoop with a broom. She swept the steps and then began on the rock walk going to the gate. "She's tall, Granny Hutch is," freighter Millican had told Eve. "And she won't be carrying any flesh about her middle. She's up in her sixties, I reckon. Anyway, her hair's about the color of an ash heap before the sun hits it."

This had to be Granny Hutch.

A hawk screamed in the noonday sky. The woman shaded her eyes, trying to spot it. When she looked down, she saw Eve. "Child," she gasped, "where did you come from?"

"From Home of the Tyne. I'm Eve Sheldon. You must be Granny Hutch."

"Yes. Yes, I'm Granny Hutch." The bewildered look left the woman's face and surprise took over. "Home of the Tyne. Land sakes, child, that's three, four hundred miles back in East Texas."

"That's why I'm here," Eve said. She came out from behind the hollyhocks. "I wanted to come to the Hill Country so much that I rode a hay truck with two freighters."

"Jim Millican, most likely," Granny Hutch muttered.

"That was his name," Eve said eagerly. "The other man was a Mr. Morgan."

For a moment Granny Hutch leaned against her broom. She straightened then and said sharply, "You come out of my flower bed and you talk." She looked at Eve. "Why didn't Jim Millican take you on to Marty and send you back by bus?"

"He said you needed me."

"Drat him." Granny Hutch flung open the yard gate. "Come on. We'll get my pickup truck and run him down."

Eve ran after her. "We can't catch him," she said. "I know he can't drive the hay truck fast but I've been here hiding in your hollyhocks for almost an hour."

Granny Hutch turned on her. "Hiding," she said sharply, "Why?"

Eve's mouth quivered. "I was afraid," she said.

"Well, my land. Come on to the kitchen. It's hot out here in the noonday sun."

They went up the walk. "We were playing Hide-and-seek at the Home," Eve explained. "I hid behind a lilac bush by the street. Two truckers had stopped there. They were fixing a wheel. I heard them talking about going to the Hill Country, and how they drove in the cool of the night. When I got a chance, I crawled under the hay on the truck bed. They didn't find me till the next morning."

At the door Granny Hutch asked, "Why come to the Hill Country?"

"My parents were coming to the Hill Country. They had a car wreck. Both of them were killed. I was a baby, and I had no relatives. That's why I grew up in the Home."

A look of pain crossed Granny Hutch's face. "For a moment there," she said, "I thought you were Cindy come back to life."

Eve said, "Mr. Millican told me how Cindy came to

live with you after you were left alone. Then Cindy died."

"Don't," Granny Hutch whispered. She led Eve through the front door into tthe kitchen where a cedar bucket hanging by the east window floated a gourd dipper. A long eating table was spaced between the front door and a door to the bedroom. Why, this is something out of the past, Eve thought, no electricity, no running water. I'd love it here, I would.

Granny Hutch pulled a chair from against the wall and sat. "Come here," she told Eve. "Let me look at you."

Eve stood awkwardly. "I'm not much to see," she said. "I'm skinny and freckled. Right now I'm dirty."

"Yes," Granny Hutch said absently. "Yes, I can see all that. What I can't see is what I'm going to do with you."

"Mr. Millican said that you needed another girl."

Eve looked at the big fireplace. It looked friendly. A great wave of longing came over her. "Please, Granny Hutch," she begged, "couldn't I live with you?"

"No." Granny Hutch spoke firmly. "And if that Jim Millican hadn't been an ornery old bachelor I'd haul you right down to Marty. I'd drop you out on him the same way he dropped you out on me."

Suddenly Eve saw wildflowers through the front door. "Indian daisies beside the creek," she breathed. "At the Home, Miss Woodruff taught us about wildflowers, but we never got to see them grow."

"That's Dog Branch, where I get my water,"

Granny Hutch said. "And folks around here call these red-flowered weeds Indian blankets. But it's past noon. Wash up in that pan by the water bucket. I'll put the greens and corn pone on the table."

An iron dinner pot hung from a hook in the fire-place. It held turnip greens with a chunk of sidemeat. A pone of cornbread still smoked when Granny Hutch lifted the Dutch oven lid. She emptied the greens to a bowl. She handed the pot with its juice to Eve. "After I've said the blessing, crumble your corn pone into the juice. Folks here call that pot likker."

Eve's eyes danced when she tasted the food. "That," she said, "is pure ambrosia."

"Ambrosia?"

"That's what King Solomon fed to the Queen of Sheba."

Granny Hutch buttered her cornbread soberly. "Well," she said, "he'd have liked pot likker a sight better."

They washed the dishes. Granny Hutch brought her comb and brush from the bedroom. "Come here," she told Eve. "I'm going to comb the hay out of your hair. My land, it's pretty brown hair, just begging to curl."

She sat and put Eve between her knees. She began to brush. "Tomorrow," she said, "I'll scrounge around and find you a change of clothes. We need to wash what you have on."

Happiness flooded Eve. "Then you'll keep me?" she asked.

"No. But while you're here, you'll be clean. Sure,

you'll get dirty working. But what gets scrubbed off at night is just dirt. What stays on for a month is filth. I don't hold to filth."

She finished Eve's hair and went to the bedroom. "Here's my spare bonnet," she said when she came out. "Put it on. I'll get a couple of hoes from the corncrib. We'll hoe the watermelons while you're here to help."

The big bonnet had a high crown. The headpiece was stuffed with cardboard strips to hold its shape. Eve said, "I've never worn a bonnet before."

"Put it on," Granny Hutch said. "Chances are you've never hoed melons either." She went out the door.

Suddenly Eve was afraid again. If Granny Hutch sees I've never had a hoe in my hand, she thought, will she send me right back? She looked through the open kitchen door. The sky above Dog Branch was a blue tent. "Please, God," she whispered, "show me what to cut up at the melon patch and what to leave. Can't you see how it is? I've just got to stay." She went down the walk to where Granny Hutch waited at the gate. Together they walked to the melon patch.

The vines had big melons. There weren't any weeds, just grass to hoe. "Come Fourth of July," Granny Hutch said, "I aim to take ripe melons to the Marty Reunion. Reckon I've been right lucky getting showers. Lots of folks lost their melon crops from drought." She watched Eve's awkward hoeing. "Have you ever seen a patch of melons growing?" she asked.

"Oh, no. Just things growing in yards and parks."

12

Granny Hutch smiled grimly. "Sink your hoe under that whole grass tuft. Get it out. root and all. You don't kill grass by cutting off the top."

Eve hoed on. I still can't get it out of my mind, she thought, that here time has turned backward. I always dreamed of living somewhere where there'd be no noise of cars nor airplanes, some place where water was dipped, not piped; some place where I could light a lamp or eat biscuits from a Dutch oven. I didn't know such a place existed now. She smiled. I did see a summer school bus, she thought, and Granny Hutch spoke of having a truck. Guess that's modern.

2

They hoed to the east end of the field and back. Granny Hutch had brought a jug of water. Now she lifted it from between the roots of a postoak. It was Eve's first time to drink from a jug. Never had water tasted so good.

A covey of quail came out of the bunch grass at the edge of the field. Eve watched them step about proudly. "They're talking their heads off," she whispered to Granny Hutch. "Look how they puff out their little chests. Oh my, they think they're worth a million. What kind of birds are they?"

"Quail," Granny Hutch whispered back. "Folks around here call them bobwhite."

Eve corked the jug. Carefully she set it back between the postoak roots, making no noise. "Why are they named bobwhites?" she asked.

"It's their call, I guess. Lean a little closer. I'll whisper an old rhyme I heard when I was a child:

> 'Bobwhite, Bobwhite, are your peas all right?
> No, Bobwhite, not quite, not quite.
> Come back tomorrow night,
> And we'll all take a bite.'"

A yell ripped through the trees. It was gutteral at first, then suddenly it rose shrilly, like rocks skipping across water. Eve jumped a melon vine and caught Granny Hutch's arm. The quail flew off with a great whirring sound.

"It's all right," Granny Hutch said. "It's just my neighbor John Devvies. That's his Rebel yell."

The yell came nearer through the trees. Eve's voice quavered. "What's a Rebel yell?"

Granny Hutch said, "The Confederate soldiers used it during the Civil War. John Devvies learned it from his great-grandfather. He uses it when his wife Viry nags him too much."

A man followed by four hounds came out of the woods. He was tall and bent forward at the waist. Like a man who can't get where he's going fast enough, Eve thought.

"You Liver Pill," Granny Hutch yelled at the lead hound, "get out of my melons." She stooped quickly and came up with a rock. It caught Liver Pill on the rump. The hound yelped, clamped his tail, and ran through Granny Hutch's melons. Eve giggled. He's not really hurt, she decided. He's just putting on.

The other hounds joined in the bawling. All four went round and round among the melon vines.

Granny Hutch shook a finger at the man behind the hounds. "John Devvies," she yelled.

"Why, howdy, neighbor," John Devvies said.

"John Devvies, get your pesky dogs out of my melons before they rip my vines to pieces. Get them out. Do you hear?"

John Devvies grinned happily. "Sure, Granny Hutch. Sure. My hounds mind me." He turned on Liver Pill. "Get out of Granny Hutch's melons," he yelled. All four hounds dropped to the ground and lay like dead. "Or on the ground, one." He saw Eve. "Why, bless me," he said, "who's this?"

"She's Eve Sheldon," Granny Hutch said. "That dratted Jim Millican dropped her off on me. He knows good and well I don't need her."

"Oh, don't you?" John Devvies came over to Eve. He's sizing me up, Eve thought. She had to laugh.

John Devvies went around Eve, looking her over the way he would have sized up a stray hound. "Well now," he said finally, "I reckon she'd be a sight of help once you got her filled up." His blue eyes sparkled with fun as he looked at Eve. Eve smiled back at him. She felt that she had a friend in Granny Hutch's wild neighbor.

Granny Hutch spoke up. "Now, John Devvies, I don't aim to keep that child. Jim Millican didn't have a bit of business dropping her off on me like he would a stray cat. The first chance I get, I'm sending her back to the Home."

"So that's where she came from," John Devvies said. He glared at Granny Hutch. "You'd send a little bitty orphan girl off just because you're too stubborn to own up you need her?"

Granny Hutch glared back at him.

Eve wandered off to where a huge granite boulder stood on the other side of the postoak. They're not really mad at each other, she decided. I bet they have a good time when they get to arguing.

Man's Head was what Granny Hutch had told her the big boulder was named. It was hollow in the middle. Eve put her head inside its cavern. She called out to Granny Hutch and John Devvies. She liked the way her voice rang.

"You be careful of rattlesnakes," Granny Hutch said. She and John Devvies came over to the boulder. "If a rattlesnake's coiled up in that rock," she warned Eve, "it'll take the same color as the granite."

"There's not any rattlesnake," Eve said. "But there's some little moss growing inside the hollow." She came out into the late sun holding a tiny plant. "It's prairie stonecrop," she said in wonder. "I've never seen it growing before, but I've studied its picture. And I've read all about it." She touched the bit of moss gently. Her face still held its wonder. Suddenly, as if to herself, she began to quote:

> "'Flower in the crannied wall,
> I pluck you out of the crannies,
> I hold you here, root and all, in my hand.
> Little flower—but *if* I could understand
> What you are, root and all, and all in all,
> I should know what God and man is.'"

Slowly John Devvies reached for his red cap. He tucked it under his arm. His face was solemn as he looked at Eve. "That," he said, "is the prettiest set of words I ever heard. Did you just make them up?"

"No, Mr. Devvies. A man named Tennyson wrote them."

John Devvies shook his head. "Never knew a preacher at camp meeting to say words prettier. I declare, girl, when you said them you had a look of pure glory on your face."

"Well," Granny Hutch said drily, "judging by the sun it's time to milk Old Rose and feed the shoat. And I don't know of any set of pretty words that'll do it either."

John Devvies whistled to his dogs. They came to life and tore through the vines to where he stood. At the edge of the melon patch he looked back at Eve. This time there was no devilment in his eyes as he said, "Goodbye, Glory Girl."

When they reached the cabin Granny Hutch got the milk bucket. Eve followed her to the pen where a dark red cow waited, her udder full and dripping. Granny Hutch drove her in and opened the calf pasture gate to let her calf in. She lifted down the milking stool from the rail fence. "Oh," said Eve, "I'm going to learn how to milk Old Rose."

"You won't be staying," Granny Hutch reminded her.

When she got up from the stool the bucket was full. "Get six ears of corn from the crib," she told Eve. "Shuck them for the mare Bess in the horse lot. She's a heap of help to me places where I can't drive the pickup. Then throw six little nubbins to the shoat."

Eve heard the big gray mare whinnying for her corn. She left off husking the ears until she could go out and pet her. When she went back to the corncrib, she was more determined to stay than ever. I haven't given up, she thought as she watched Old Bess nibble her corn. Please, God, couldn't you figure out some way for Granny Hutch to keep me?

When Eve reached the kitchen Granny Hutch set out the remainder of the cornbread and greens. She added a glass of milk at each plate. They ate and washed the dishes.

The moon rode the treetops. Granny Hutch got one of her nightgowns and a towel from the wardrobe. She took Eve out on the stoop and pointed toward the creek.

"See that clump of liveoaks on the far side of Dog Branch," she told Eve. "There's a pool rimmed with granite rocks there. A fine place to bathe. Here's a hunk of lye soap. Mind you, though, you look out for rattlesnakes."

Around the cabin the hills lay silver blue now with moonlight. Granny Hutch turned to go inside. Eve stopped her. "Don't you hear them, Granny Hutch?" she asked.

"Hear what?'

"The hills. They're singing. Such a soft little tune. Don't you hear it?"

"Well," said Granny Hutch, "I don't reckon I ever heard a hill sing. But if John Devvies could see you now he'd declare you had that glory look again."

It was fun for Eve to walk down the dirt trail and to feel the summer dust powder her feet. It was fun to wade out into Dog Branch. The water gurgled around her. Little minnows bit her toes. She could see them, and their tickling bites made her laugh. Finally she came to the pool. Why, it's a real bathtub, she thought. Only it's got granite rocks for is sides. She scrubbed happily. She hadn't realized how much she missed the nightly baths at the Home.

She laid the yellow lye soap on a smooth rock where the water barely trickled. Moonlight shone straight down on it. It looked to Eve exactly like a bar of gold.

Stillness lay over everything. But that was the way it had to be, Eve knew. If the crickets and frogs and all the little live things made their noises, she couldn't possibly hear the singing hills.

She waded out to a rock on the bank to put on Granny Hutch's nightgown. It was too long and of such a coarse weave it felt scratchy. But it had a clean, dry smell.

She walked slowly back to the cabin. She had to be careful and not dirty her feet. An owl hooted from the liveoaks. She thought of the cot Granny Hutch had set up for her to sleep on. The owl gave another muffled hoot, as if its head were down in its neck feathers. Eve thought of Miss Woodruff and of the boys and girls at the Home. "I don't want to go back," she said to the owl, "but I do wish Granny Hutch would let me sleep in the big bed with her. I bet Cindy did."

3

"I declare," Granny Hutch grumbled two mornings later as Eve hopped out of bed and ran to the window, "You've got energy like you're charged with some kind of power."

"Can't help it," Eve declared. She drew herself up in the long night dress. "See how tall I am in your nightgown? I've grown since I've come here." She looked out the window in the half light. "Wonder what today will bring," she said. "I've been here two whole days. Both were different. There's always excitement outside."

She pulled on her dress. She didn't bother with shoes now. Her feet had become the color of brown sand rock. She came over to where Granny Hutch sat tiredly on the side of her bed. "Wonder what will happen today?" she asked again.

"The milking, most likely," Granny Hutch said crossly. "Then slopping the pig. Carrying him water to wallow in next. Feeding the chickens. I reckon if you stretched your mind enough you could call that excitement."

Eve laughed. She ran to kindle a fire in the fireplace. The Dutch oven had to heat. "Maybe we'll find a redbird's nest in the shinoak by the tumbled down rock fence," she called back to Granny Hutch. "Or maybe some strange kind of flower blooming on Dog Branch." She stirred up cornmeal batter and sang:

"Cornbread's in the oven,
Bacon's in the skillet,
Water bucket's empty,
Gotta go fill it."

She danced out of the cabin with the empty cedar bucket. She was happy because Granny Hutch was smiling a little.

I'll help her, Eve thought as she skipped down to Dog Branch. I'll be such help that finally she can't do without me. She looked up at the pale morning sky. "Now, God," she said, "I want to thank you that I learned to cook at the Home. Also, I want to ask you not to let anybody come along to take me back to the Home. I'm going to try everything I know to stay here. Then too, God, I know you don't approve of tricks. But please don't let Granny Hutch find that dollar Mr. Millican gave me. It's under my cot mattress. I'm keeping it till Christmas. Oh, yes, I plan to be here then. That dollar buys Granny Hutch a Christmas present."

She hurried on. She did hope that she hadn't tired God with that long talk.

A mockingbird broke out in such a melody that the liveoaks were showered with music. Eve waded out into the swift water. She stood still, letting the minnows nibble at her feet. She looked toward the east to where the sun touched the tree line as it came up. All about her lay the new morning, hushed and waiting. "God," she said, "you sure have a pretty world."

She leaned over to catch a trickle of water in her bucket. A deer snorted up Dog Branch. Then Eve heard it crash through the shinoaks. It came toward her. "A mama deer," Eve whispered as twin fawns parted the brush. They nudged the mama doe's flanks, and their little tails wiggled happily. Such a nice easy way to live, Eve thought, dinner any time they get mama stopped.

She filled the bucket and stood up carefully. But the doe deer saw her. She cleared the short brush by Eve with one bound. The underside of her tail waved like a white flag. The twin fawns melted into the bushes. Save for a shaking of leaves, Eve could not have told they were there.

Back in the kitchen Eve hung up the bucket of water. She wrinkled her nose in pleasure. That bacon sure smelled good. Sidemeat, Granny Hutch called it. Anyway, its good smell made Eve hungry. "I hope," she said, "my breakfast doesn't run away like the fawns'." She told Granny Hutch about the deer.

"John Devvies' hounds will be sure to find them," Granny Hutch complained. "There used to be lots of wild turkey roosting on Dog Branch, but his pesky dogs have mighty nigh run them out. Reckon I've got to give that man another good talking to. He ought not to let his hounds run loose."

Eve ate her cornmeal mush. It had such a good taste that morning. "Granny Hutch," she said finally, "you like John Devvies as a neighbor. I just know you do."

Granny Hutch went over to the Dutch oven. She scooped up two wedges of crisp cornbread. "Well," she said, putting a wedge on Eve's plate, "I reckon John Devvies is the best neighbor and the aggravatingest man I know. Sometimes I get so mad at him I can't see. He waits till I'm right in the middle of giving him fits. Then he grins at me and hands me a dozen eggs, a jar of sugared molasses, or just anything I can eat. A body would think maybe I went hungry." She reached for the molasses pitcher. "If his wife Viry ever finds out he's giving me vittles, she'll have a regular duck fit."

Eve said, "You never did tell me much about Viry. What's she like?"

Granny Hutch drank her coffee thoughtfully. "Reckon you'll be going back to the Home before you see her," she said, "but that woman's got a tongue forked as a snake's. Forever on to her husband about something."

"Does Mr. Devvies quarrel with her?"

"Oh, no. John Devvies never rightly quarreled with anybody. But when I look out the door and see his pickup coming so fast it's plowing ground, I know. Why, when he comes by like that you'd declare the whole San Saba Mob was chasing him. But he's just tearing out to Marty because he can't stand Viry's tongue another minute."

Eve got up to stack the dishes. "I like him," she said. "I don't want Viry tongue lashing him, but I do hope that he comes by every few days."

Granny Hutch took down the dishpan where it hung on the kitchen wall. "Eve," she said, "I can't seem to make you understand. If I can rake up enough money by the time John Devvies goes back to Marty, I'm sending you along with him so you can take the bus back to the Home. Whoever comes by after I've got the money, I'm sending you back."

"Oh," said Eve, "If you're going to send me back, I hope that Mr. Devvies doesn't come by."

Granny Hutch spoke as if to herself, "I just may not be able to get enough money together," she said.

About noon Eve got her first sight of John Devvies' battered red pickup truck. She ran to the north door. The pickup truck was topping the hill. The running gear lay low to the ground as the pickup fairly plowed dirt.

John Devvies sat hunched on the edge of the seat. He rode the ground bumps like a granite rock being pulled along. His left hand steered the truck. His right hand waved in the breeze. The pickup careened first on the right wheels then it flopped over on the left. Every so often he took his hand off the steering wheel to mash the horn until it emitted a long, mournful sound.

Eve turned to Granny Hutch. She had two big questions in her eyes.

"Guess he's had a tongue fight with Viry," Granny Hutch said. "John Devvies told me he hoped Viry went to heaven, but he sure hoped her temper went some place else."

On came the pickup. The front wheels seemed to lift as they topped the hill. Then John Devvies slammed on the brakes and they touched ground again. "Hip, hip," he yelled. Then, "Hup, hup." His big body bent over the steering wheel. Eve thought that he looked for all the world like a double-jointed doll she once had at the Home.

Suddenly Eve giggled. "He sure acts tough," she told Granny Hutch, "but really he isn't. When he gets too wild I notice he slams on the brakes." She grabbed Granny Hutch's arm. "Look," she said. "The hounds are riding in the pickup bed, all four of them. Will they go with him to Marty?"

"I wish they would," Granny Hutch grumbled, "but they won't. They'll go a ways. Then they'll jump out to nose my slop bucket."

John Devvies swung the truck around the corner of the yard fence and Eve's happiness fled. Oh, she thought, if he stops I'll have to go with him to Marty and take the bus.

John Devvies jumped out of the truck and slammed the door with a bang. Then he stamped up the walk and through the open kitchen door. The hounds jumped out of the truck bed and followed him.

Granny Hutch put her hands on her hips. "You John Devvies," she said, "here I just got through scrubbing my kitchen floor. Now look at it. I could trail every hound you've got by his tracks."

The hounds kept padding about the kitchen.

"Just you say the word," John Devvies told Granny Hutch. "Just one little bitsy word and I'll make my dogs quit your kitchen like a whirlwind. They mind me, these hounds do. A sight better'n most folks' young'uns mind." He turned on the dogs so fast that Liver Pill stopped by the kitchen table. One forepaw was still in the air.

"Get outta this house," John Devvies yelled.

All four hounds split the breeze through the middle door. They scooted under Granny Hutch's bed and lay there like dead.

"Or under the bed, one," said John Devvies.

He brushed his big hands together. Then he remembered and whipped off his red cap. Politely he stashed it under his left arm. "Now, Mrs. Hutch," he said, "what be you needing from Marty?"

Granny Hutch got her tablet and pencil from behind the mantel clock. "I need several things," she told him, "but in order to have enough cash money I'd have to send my eggs. Only I can't send them because of the way you drive. Mr. Klett won't buy scrambled eggs."

John Devvies sat on the edge of his chair while Granny Hutch made out her list. Presently he spied Eve sorting clothes in the bedroom. He looked off fast, pretending not to see her. Then he darted another quick look and another. Eve was already giggling over the hounds under Granny Hutch's bed. Now she laughed outright.

"Good morning, Mr. Devvies," she said.

John Devvies all but jumped out of his chair. He reached up to take off his cap. Then he remembered. "Howdy, Glory Girl," he drawled. "Thought sure Granny Hutch would have taken the broom and run you off by now. She aiming to let you stay?"

"No, I'm not letting her stay," Granny Hutch said firmly. "If I had a mite more money I could send her to Marty with you." She looked a bit wishful at John

Devvies. "Reckon I'll have to wait till I go in and take my eggs."

John Devvies didn't look at her. "Reckon you will," he said. He tucked Granny Hutch's bill in his shirt pocket and took the money she handed him. "I'm right glad you don't have enough cash money," he said. "I sure would miss Glory Girl here if she went back to the Home."

Granny Hutch whirled on him. "Maybe you'd like to take her to live with you and Viry."

John Devvies looked sober. "Wish I could," he said. "But you know my Viry. I'd bring this little bitty girl along and she'd throw a yelling fit. Besides, you need her."

"John Devvies, I don't need anybody."

John Devvies winked at Eve. "Glad to hear it, Granny. Glad to hear it. But Glory Girl needs you. So I reckon you'll keep her."

"You haven't heard me say I'll keep her."

Eve saw right away that John Devvies meant to tease Granny Hutch until dinner was on the table. Then she'd have to ask him to eat. Eve hurried to heat the Dutch oven while she beat up the biscuit dough.

At the table Granny Hutch said the blessing. Then she passed John Devvies the ham and gravy. John Devvies didn't even notice. He was eyeing Eve's tiny biscuits. He picked one up and held it between his thumb and forefinger. "Now that's something," he said. "I bet Glory Girl cut them out with a thimble. Why, my Viry's biscuits are big as saucers. Trouble is she hurries them too much. A biscuit's just naturally got to squat before it can rise. But Viry gets in a fizz and bakes hers on the squat." His big hand closed over the plate of biscuits. "I'll just take six or seven of these little fellers," he said.

Later John Devvies took off for town at such a pace that Granny Hutch declared it gave her a headache. The hounds came to life under the bed. All four made a beeline through the kitchen door and out the front gate. Their yelps floated back so high and keening that Granny Hutch sat down and threw her apron over her head. "Land a living," she cried, "they sound like bench mourners at a camp meeting."

In the middle of her laughing Eve stopped. "Sh-h-h," she whispered to Granny Hutch. "Mama bird's out in the postoak teaching her babies to fly."

Granny Hutch hurried to the window. "They've all gone but the littlest one," she whispered. "See how its wings droop and its tail upends. It doesn't want to go, but the mama bird will push it out if it doesn't fly."

They watched the baby bird fall to the ground. "Oh, how could she push it out," said Eve.

Granny Hutch was quiet for a long time. Then she said, "I may have to do like the mama bird. If you won't be willing to go back to the Home, I may have to push you out."

Eve's face went white. "Is it because of Cindy?"

"Partly. But it's other things, too. Old Rose might fail her milk. The shoat might sicken and die before I could butcher it for meat. The hens might stop laying. At the Home, eating was part of the day's pattern. Even wild creatures know how to stay with the pattern of things. I don't want to be hard. But I don't want you to go hungry either."

There was a willow down by the tumbled rock fence. Eve ran to it. She climbed the middle branch as high as she could go. She rode it to the ground and up again. I've got to do something, she thought. If I don't, I'm going to cry. She came back to the ground, kicked, and let the branch fling her high once more.

This is fun, Eve thought. Anyway, it beats crying.

The moon came up. It silvered the rock fence. Still Eve swung. An armadillo lumbered along. It stopped at the roots of the willow to hunt for bugs and lice. Granny Hutch called from the cabin. "Eve, come in. A rattlesnake might bite you. Do you hear me?"

Yes, I hear you, Eve thought. But I don't hear you say what I want you to say. John Devvies wouldn't let us starve. I can't take Cindy's place, but I'd make a place for myself.

"Eve, do you hear me?"

She slid off the willow limb and watched it straighten. Then she ran toward the kitchen light.

4

The following Sunday they washed the breakfast dishes quietly. Eve had her mind on ways of persuading Granny Hutch to keep her. Granny Hutch had her mind some place else. Eve wondered where.

Presently Granny Hutch said, "We'll go to Cindy's grave this morning. I always go on Sundays."

Eve said, "I wondered when you'd take me."

Granny Hutch answered slowly, "I've never taken anybody there."

"Oh, but I've been there," Eve said. "And on moonlight nights I see it when I bathe."

She stopped and looked at Granny Hutch shyly. "I've gone up the steps to the top of the wall around it, but I've never gone on down. I didn't think I ought to unless you told me so."

Granny Hutch brought their bonnets from the bedroom. "Going to Cindy's grave on Sunday," she said, "is like going to church." She put on her bonnet and got the broom.

"You go out to the smokehouse and get the hoe," she told Eve. "Some weeds might have come up."

They walked toward Dog Branch. The sun hid behind a cloud. A wind sprang up. It riffled the red Indian daisies. Eve wanted to sing and dance. It was that kind of morning. She walked quietly, though, because Granny Hutch looked sad.

Granny Hutch spoke. "On Sundays, I take Mr. Hutch's family Bible from the top wardrobe shelf. But it's a chore for me to read. I never got much schooling. That's one of the main reasons I'm sending you back. A body needs schooling." Presently she asked, "Can you read the Bible?"

"Oh, yes," said Eve. "At Home of the Tyne we took turns reading every morning. I always loved reading the Song of Solomon, especially where it says the voice of the turtle is heard on the land."

"Never could make that out," Granny Hutch answered. "Turtles don't really have voices."

"Oh, but they do. Everything has a voice. Even the wildflowers have voices. You just listen good and hard. You'll hear all kinds of voices."

Granny Hutch shook her head. "I declare," she said, "you do talk the strangest things. Sometimes I don't rightly know what to say to you."

You could say you want to keep me, Eve thought. You could say you'd give me a home. I'd learn how to do your kind of work. She smiled to herself. I've already learned how to hoe weeds, she thought.

The flats along Dog Branch were orange-yellow now with the Texas coreopsis. Eve said, "You'd think they hunted up every brush pile in the pasture and bloomed there. I love the way they peep out at us. They're so tall and graceful."

"What'd you call them?" Granny Hutch asked.

"Coreopsis."

"Well, I always thought they were just yellow-flowered weeds."

"When I walk with Old Bess," Eve said, "I tell her what Miss Woodruff taught us was the real Texas coreopsis. It has a circle of reddish brown marks at the base of its petals. I show them to Old Bess as we traipse along." Eve liked the sound of the word traipse. She'd heard Granny Hutch use it.

Granny Hutch said, "Now I bet that mare sure knows what you're talking about." She looked at Eve and frowned. "I declare," she said, "you're brown as a pecan stick, and all scratched up with briars. I didn't know you'd been following old Bess around."

They crossed the stepping stones over Dog Branch. Eve like the way the gravel under their feet felt coarse and crunchy, especially as they stepped out on the other side.

They came to Cindy's grave. It was enclosed by a slab-rock wall. Steps led to the top and down the other side.

Eve stopped her chattering as if she were entering a sanctuary. She started up the steps. Half way to the top she turned to Granny Hutch. Her face wore a kind of hushed look. Granny Hutch looked at her. But Eve knew by her face that she meant yes. She went on down the steps.

She carried a limp bouquet of the coreopsis with her. She laid the flowers against the headstone. Then she began pulling the new crop of sandburs covering the mound. "I wish Cindy could have lived," she said. "We would have had fun."

Granny Hutch climbed to the top step. She handed down the broom and hoe. "I built this wall myself," she said, "out of that old rock fence. I carved the headstone with Cindy's name on it. I thought maybe by working hard like that I'd be able to sleep come nights. But I couldn't. Not for a long time."

Gently Eve brushed the mound with the broom. "I know what Cindy was to you," she said. "She was the stars and the moon and the sun, all rolled into one."

"And I don't ever aim to love anybody that way again," Granny Hutch said firmly, and turned away. Silently Eve climbed over the wall and hurried to catch up with her.

As they crossed Dog Branch Eve said, "Granny Hutch, did you ever play a game called Tug-O-War?"

"Seems like I did. When I was a child. That's where somebody draws a line. A child takes one end of the rope. Another child takes the other end. They stretch the rope across the line and pull."

"That's the game. And the child who pulls the other child across the line wins." Eve skipped up beside Granny Hutch. "You and I are playing that game," she said. "You're trying to pull me across the line so you can send me back to the Home. I'm trying to pull you across so I can stay. God's on the line."

"Eve," Granny Hutch gasped, "you oughtn't say such things about God."

"But God's everyplace, isn't he?"

"Yes. Yes, come to think of it, he is."

"Then he can be at the middle of our rope. He'll decide who wins."

Granny Hutch kept shaking her head. "Eve," she said, "never did anybody foul up my thinking the way you do."

They crossed the flats of yellow coreopsis and came to the cabin.

Even Bible reading didn't bring Granny Hutch back from wherever her mind had taken her. The day was all too quiet for Eve. Granny Hutch doesn't want me, she thought. She went out and sat on the stoop. She could see the big elm where Cindy's grave was. Eve's thoughts ran on: She still wants Cindy. Why can't she want me? I couldn't be Cindy, but I could be *something*.

There was the willow. She would swing on it for awhile. She jumped off the stoop and ran toward it.

The setting sun made a rosy backdrop. Eve swung far out on the middle limb. She tried to see just how high it would fling her against a background of hill and sky and rock fence. Up in the air she went. She could feel her long plaits standing straight out behind her. The limb brought her down. Her plaits slapped hard against her back.

From the kitchen window Granny Hutch called her to supper.

The meal was quiet. Eve spooned brown sugar across her mush. Somehow, though, she didn't enjoy its taste. She didn't drink her milk right down. She just sipped it.

Granny Hutch said, "When I went to the window

to call you to supper you were hanging scandalously far out on that willow limb. Simply out over nothing. It fair took my breath to see you hanging so high. What makes you swing on that willow?"

Over the rim of her cup Eve's eyes searched Granny Hutch's. Then she smiled. "It's a way of bouncing off my misery," she said. "I wish you had a way of bouncing off yours."

"Misery, child. Why, what misery do you have? Do I work you too hard? Are you lonesome, maybe, to go back to the Home?"

Eve was shocked. "Go back?" she cried. "I don't ever want to leave here. The misery I have is because you don't want to keep me."

Granny Hutch looked out the window so long that Eve held her breath. Have I said too much, she wondered.

Still Granny sat. The evening kept stretching until the chimney shadow reached the yard fence. Finally Granny Hutch said, "You can stay till I have some watermelons to sell. I won't have enough money till then. I'll get some pretty print and make you a dress. That way, you can ride the bus back like quality folks. I won't have the Home thinking I'm poor white trash."

"Will it be soon?" Eve asked.

"Never can tell about a patch of watermelons. One day you think they'll be ready in a week. Next day you can't be sure. Anyway, you have to go to school somewhere when school starts in the fall."

"But I'm getting such a good education here," Eve said. "I've learned things I never could have learned in the schoolroom. Besides, the Marty school bus comes within a mile.''

Granny Hutch said firmly, ''I know the school bus comes close enough for you to catch it at the big road. But sending you to school will take money. The Home was doing a fine job educating you and doing it free.''

That night Eve couldn't sleep. Maybe the melons would be slow getting ripe. Maybe Granny Hutch would see how much she was learning right there and how much she was helping with the work. Maybe she wouldn't send her back after all.

Granny Hutch snored softly in the big bed. The sound soothed Eve. It was like a kind of little tune. Eve turned over on the cot and went to sleep.

"Eve, for heaven sakes, wake up." Granny Hutch
shook Eve again as she lay all doubled up on her cot.
"Now get up," she said.

Eve sat up. Her plaits were a fuzzy tousle. Her eyes
were wide with excitement. "I was having a dream,"
she said. "I was nearly to the top of that tall pecan tree
with the crane's nest." She sat on the side of the cot
and pulled on her dress. "Then the wind began calling,
'Eve, wake up.'" She yawned and laughed. "It wasn't
the wind calling and shaking me after all. It was you."

Granny Hutch spoke a bit kinder. "We did do a
heap of work yesterday. I reckon you were right tuck-
ered out when you went to bed."

Eve slid off the cot. She ran across the splintered
floor. "Look through the window," she told Granny
Hutch. "Day's pointing its finger at us. It says hurry
and come outside."

Granny Hutch said firmly, "Tomorrow's the
Fourth of July. We'll pull a load of ripe melons before
the sun comes up. Then we'll take them to the Marty
Reunion."

All the built-in excitement went out of Eve. "You mean," she said slowly, "that when you sell the melons I have to take the bus back to the Home?"

"Eve," Granny Hutch said as she poured their breakfast mush, "I've been doing a heap of figuring. Some nights I walk the floor, just thinking. But I can't keep you. I tell you, and I tell you."

"I know. Still I keep hoping." Eve smiled at Granny Hutch. "I do a lot of thinking too."

"What if the winter's a bad one?" Granny Hutch went on. "We might not have enough to eat."

"Oh, but John Devvies wouldn't let us go hungry. I just know he wouldn't."

"I won't be beholden to John Devvies or anybody else."

Eve was silent. Presently some of her excitement came back. "Let's not talk about it," she said. "Let's think about driving to Marty. Let's think about peeking in the show windows at all the pretty things. I do wish I could have a stick of striped peppermint when we get to Marty."

Granny Hutch softened. "I think I can manage that," she said.

"Before we go," Eve told her, "could I have an envelope and a stamp and a sheet of tablet paper? I want to write Miss Woodruff. I won't tell her where I am, but I don't want her worrying."

Granny Hutch hunted them up. "Likely as not," she warned, "you'll reach the Home before the letter will."

They went to the cowpen. While Granny Hutch

milked, Eve fed Old Bess and the shoat. The chickens flew into the shoat's pen and helped themselves to corn kernels.

They turned Old Rose and her calf together. They would be spending the night at the Marty Reunion, Granny Hutch said. Eve began asking questions the moment Granny Hutch headed the pickup toward the melon patch. "Where are the reunion grounds?" she wanted to know.

"They're at a big pecan grove about a mile out of Marty."

"Why is it called the Marty Reunion?"

"The old settlers around Marty are getting fewer every year. Folks have these reunions chiefly to honor them."

Eve had a few more questions. "What does everybody do at the reunion?"

"Oh, there's the Brown String Band to play when the Marty orchestra gets tired. And where the orchestra plays modern tunes the Brown Band plays old tunes for the old, old settlers—tunes like 'Silver Threads Among the Gold' or maybe 'When You and I Were Young, Maggie.' "

They came to the melon patch. Granny Hutch guided the pickup between the rows. "Down on the reunion grounds," she went on, "there'll be a hobby horse. Then tonight when the baseball game is over there'll be fireworks on the ball ground. Tomorrow there'll be a free barbecue to celebrate the Glorious Fourth. Now let's get to pulling melons before the dew dries on them."

"What does the dew do for a melon, Granny Hutch?"

"Law me, but you're full of questions. A melon has a milky crust put there by the dew. It's a kind of a protection. You handle a melon easy like while that crust's on it, and it'll stay fresh for hours."

Eve shook her head as they walked among the vines. "I just don't see how God figured it all out," she said.

"See this little curl on the vine," Granny Hutch told her. "If it's dead, chances are the melon's ripe. But a body better thump a melon just to make sure. Now you thump one. If it says *plank*, *plank*, it's green. If it says *plunk*, *plunk*, it's ripe."

Eve bent to thump a long, striped melon. "Hear it talking, Granny Hutch? It says:

Plank, plank,
Do not yank."

She moved to the next vine. "Now listen to this:

Plunk, plunk,
Have a hunk."

They went on pulling melons. Presently Eve asked, "Granny Hutch, did you ever live in a glory world?"

"A glory world. Sakes alive, what's that?"

"A glory world lives inside you. It has a tune. But you don't hear the tune. You just feel it."

"Well," Granny Hutch said tiredly, "what I feel right now is the sun. It's boring between my shoulders like a red hot iron. We're all loaded. Let's go to the cabin and get dressed."

The sun had cleared the hills by the time they left

for Marty. Now it came bearing down on them. The wet tarp covering the melons gave off a kind of steam from the pickup bed. Granny Hutch pushed back her hat of black straw. Eve sat hunched on the seat beside her. There was so much to see and to hear in the pastures they drove through.

Granny Hutch frowned at Eve's brown skirt and white blouse. She had been wearing them the day she came. "Eve," she said, "I wish you had better to wear."

"Why, this is fine," Eve said, "only you've got them all starched and ironed till I'm afraid to wiggle. I might get a wrinkle."

The road wound like a cow trail. Now they were in a bottom where native pecans grew. Wild hog plums massed in thickets by the roadside. "Look," said Eve, "the little plums are about the size of my thumb. Some of them are red, but most of them are still pink."

"They make fine jelly," Granny Hutch said. "But a body better be careful about picking them. Rattlesnakes like to coil under plum thickets where it's cool."

They stopped the pickup at a roadside spring to eat. Down below it the water ran off in an uncertain stream. Some animal had rooted out a pool below the spring. "Somebody's meat hog," Granny Hutch decided.

Somehow, as they ate their bacon sandwiches and drank the cool buttermilk, Eve kept thinking about Old Bess back at home. She kept thinking how she loved to watch the mare eat, how she'd wiggle her lips to pick up the grains then lift her head to chew while kernels of corn dribbled from her mouth. "I wish we could have driven Old Bess and the buckboard to Marty," she said.

"Well," Granny Hutch said, "It takes a good bit of time to drive all the way to Marty in the buckboard. I used to drive it, though, before I bought the pickup truck. I reckon I still miss taking Old Bess everywhere I go, like I used to. But both of us were younger then." She put the picnic things back in the basket. "Reckon I ought to tell you something."

"Old Bess loves you the way I do," Eve said, not listening very much to Granny Hutch. "That's the main reason I hate to go back."

"Well," Granny Hutch said gruffly, "let's get back in the pickup."

They drove on until they could see Marty to their south. They came to a big creek. "My, what a creek," Eve said. "It's mostly sand and gravel but it's broad as a river."

"That's Comanche Creek. It's named for the Comanche Indians that used to live in the Hill Country."

They crossed the water meandering through the creek's broad gravel bed. They came out on top of a wide, steep bank. The road was deep-rutted. Eve said, "Wonder if Mr. Millican's hay truck made those deep ruts?"

"Like as not they helped," Granny Hutch said crossly. "Every time I think about that man I want to give him a good dressing down. Maybe I'll see him at the reunion. I ought to hunt up his house. Guess, though, he wouldn't be at home."

They drove into Marty. Eve got her first look at the little town. Granny Hutch had said it grew out of the settlers' need for Indian protection. "Most of Marty's high-front buildings are made of native stone," Granny Hutch said when she saw Eve's interest. "Most of the early settlers were German and they were fine stonemasons."

They drove up the street to the post office. Eve saw sidewalks of smooth cement. She saw the crepe myrtles blooming against the house walls. Ladies in colorful slack suits walked the streets. They crowded the streets until their parasols jutted against one another. But Eve wasn't too interested in the ladies. She had spied the parade entering the west side of the square. "Oh, look," she said to Granny Hutch. "Just look at all the saddle ponies. There must be a lot of cowboys in for the reunion."

"Most Hill Country ranchers still have fine saddle ponies," Granny Hutch told her. "Some keep many trucks, and some even have runways built for airplanes."

Flags flew from the high lamp posts. "Oh," said Eve, "there are Texas flags and U.S. flags, all flying together. What a wonderful flag show."

The town mayor led the parade carrying a big U.S. flag and riding a pretty white horse. Behind him came a car all decorated with bunting and carrying men of various ages. "The V.F.W.," Eve read.

Next came the horsemen, from grandfathers to tiny tots whose fat legs barely spanned the saddle. Eve hugged her knees with joy as she heard the beat of the school band bringing up the rear. This was different from any parade she had ever seen. If only the children at the Home were here!

A single buggy was in the parade. It was driven by a pretty red-haired lady. She wore a wide, floppy hat decorated with a blue silk band to match her eyes. But it was her high stepping brown mare that caught Eve's eye. The lady's mare was wearing the same kind of hat.

Eve's breath came in sharp. It was the way she breathed when she got excited. She said, "Pull over to the curb, Granny Hutch. Please do."

Before Granny Hutch got the pickup stopped, Eve had hopped out. She took off her hat. She placed it on the front of the pickup and tied its strings to the windshield wipers. She said to Granny Hutch, "I guess maybe we'll be just as stylish as the lady and her mare." She got back into the pickup, her eyes shining. "Now," she said, "we're all set for the Marty Reunion."

They came to the reunion grounds. Eve thought that she had never seen so many tall pecan trees nor so many people. Granny Hutch drove the pickup truck close to John Devvies' lemonade stand. "Guess we can park here till the mayor makes us move." she said.

A creek bordered the reunion grounds on the east then led off in a northerly direction. Eve could see little minnows wiggling in the water. It was so hot that she longed to take off her shoes and stockings and let the minnows nibble her toes as they did at Dog Branch. However, she was anxious to get back to John Devvies' lemonade stand.

She went back to the pickup to see if Granny Hutch needed anything. "Nothing but a good drink of John Devvies' lemonade," she said, rummaging around in her satchel.

John Devvies pretended not to see Eve until she had reached the counter of his stand. "Well, bless my soul," he drawled, "if it don't look like my Glory Girl." He waved his hand proudly. "What do you think of my stand?"

"I think it's fine, Mr. Devvies," Eve said, her eyes on a tall crock of lemonade.

"So you think my stand's fine, do you? Just wait till you sample my lemonade." He looked at Granny Hutch. "Well, neighbor," he said, "it's about time you came over and told me what's wrong with my stand."

Granny Hutch walked around it. "Your lumber's too green," she told him. "That counter's already bowing up."

"Now you stop looking for gripes. My counter's the foxiest one at this reunion. See how I draped it with red, white and blue bunting? Shows I'm patriotic. Yessir, real patriotic." The two glared at each other until Eve saw their eyes twinkling. They did have such good times quarreling.

She smiled as she thought of how Granny Hutch had bragged about John Devvies. "John Devvies got the lemonade concession because he bid the highest," she had told Eve. "Postmaster McKnight told me all about it. Nobody makes lemonade as good as John Devvies."

Presently John Devvies left Granny Hutch to look around and went over to the front of his stand. He itched his back against the pecan tree in the center and called:

"Fresh lemonade,
made in the shade,
stirred with a spade,
Good enough for any old maid."

Granny Hutch took off her hat. She looked at

John Devvies. "My, my," she said, "folks can hear that voice of yours clear to Marty."

They're at it again, Eve thought happily.

But they weren't. "Here," said Granny Hutch to Eve. "I've got a nickel someplace." She fished around in her worn black satchel until she came up with it. "Take this nickel and buy some lemonade."

Viry Devvies was there, stacking soiled paper cups and setting out clean ones beside the huge stone jar of lemonade.

Eve looked her over. Viry was all flowered out in a new dress of figured lawn. Eve thought she looked for all the world like a circus tent on the move. Finally Viry sniffed a greeting in their direction. Granny Hutch smiled. She whispered to Eve, "Now that Viry's man owns a concession stand, she looks on us as poor white trash."

John Devvies waved them over. A big chunk of ice floated in the middle of the lemonade crock. To Eve that chunk of floating ice was pure joy after their hot ride. "I could drink a gallon," she whispered to Granny Hutch.

"We'll have to go easy," Granny Hutch warned her. "But I just now found some more nickels in my satchel. You keep the one I gave you till later." She went up to the counter and put down the nickels for two cups of lemonade and ice.

With one swipe of his big hand John Devvies scooped up the nickels. Then he tried to give them back. "Hey," he said to Granny Hutch, "I don't want your old nickels. We're neighbors. I don't charge neighbors."

Viry whirled her circus tent around. Granny Hutch said firmly, "Neighbors or not, we pay for our drinks."

Behind her John Devvies winked at Eve. He lifted out two paper cups. He filled one and handed it to Eve. At the same time he dropped Granny Hutch's nickels into Eve's blouse pocket. Then he took a dime out of his pants pocket so fast that Eve wasn't sure that she had seen rightly. He waited until Viry turned on him. Then he dropped it into his apron pocket. He handed Granny Hutch the other paper cup of lemonade. "Two for a dime," he said, "and, Viry, you can see they're both paid for."

Eve giggled as she drank deeply of the delicious lemonade. Granny Hutch frowned fiercely at John Devvies, then drank hers.

Viry came up to Eve and started looking her over. Eve looked back. She smiled the wide, open-hearted smile she had. Viry kept looking and drying her hands. "This is Eve Sheldon," Granny Hutch said. Still Viry kept looking and drying her hands. Eve flushed and sat down on the fender of Granny Hutch's pickup. Finally she went over to Viry. "Granny Hutch says we're neighbors," she told Viry. "If we are, then I'm going to neighbor. I don't care if you won't speak to me."

"Well, I never," Viry gasped. She sailed inside the lemonade stand like a whirlwind.

"He, he, he," John Devvies laughed. Viry turned on him. He fell to stirring lemonade and singing like mad:

"Fresh lemonade,
Fresh lemonade,
Good enough for any old maid."

Night came early in the pecan grove. As soon as the last shafts of sunlight flickered through the trees, everybody moved to the baseball ground. Here were the fireworks. They were the first Eve had ever seen. She leaned heavily against Granny Hutch's knee. "It's like fairyland," she breathed. "All those gorgeous sparkling lights are like a billion fireflies turned loose."

"Yes," said Granny Hutch, "but the best is always saved to the last."

The last roman candle shot the American flag into the air. Then it snuffed out and everything was dark. Men's pipes glowed in the dark before the lights came on. Eve was so excited she scarcely could sit still. "Oh," she cried as they made their way back to the lighted grounds, "that was the prettiest man-made sight I ever saw."

"Man-made?"

"Well," Eve explained, "it wasn't God-made. Not like the sunset or a purple twilight. I call them and the moon and stars and Old Bess and Dog Branch God-made things."

They slept that night close to John Devvies and Viry who had made their bed inside the lemonade stand. Granny Hutch had driven the pickup near them and unrolled hers and Eve's bed beneath it. "Wish I'd sold out all the melons," Granny Hutch complained. "Then we could have slept in the pickup bed."

A moon rode high above the tall pecans. Eve couldn't sleep. She rolled over and watched Viry take down her hair. "Why, she's got her hair all teased up a mile high," Eve whispered astonished.

"She wears her hair that way," Granny Hutch whispered back. "It's right stylish that way, you know."

Eve listened to Viry giving John Devvies a good tongue lashing. He had let a couple of boys have free lemonade.

Again Eve whispered to Granny Hutch. "She'd be pretty if she didn't have that terrible tongue."

Granny Hutch grumbled, "One thing for sure if she didn't have such a temper John Devvies' old pickup wouldn't have to make so many trips into town. Now go to sleep."

Long before the tree shadows shortened the next morning a group of World War II veterans had lined the seats on the high grandstand. The Marty orchestra struck up "The Star-Spangled Banner." Crippled soldiers threw their caps high in the tops of the pecans and yelled. "I'm so thrilled," Eve whispered to Granny Hutch. "Still, I want to cry."

"They'll honor the old, old settlers next," Granny Hutch told her. "They're older than World War I."

Suddenly the band played "Dixie." Boys and girls danced out on the grandstand, clapped their hands, and began singing at the top of their voices. "Now I really do want to cry," Eve said. Everybody took up the refrain:

"Den I wish I was in Dixie,
Hooray, Hooray;
In Dixieland I'll take my stand
To live and die in Dixie . . ."

The whole crowd was wild now with yelling. Their noise drowned out the tune. But Eve could hear the beat of the big drum. The locked-up sadness within her went out. She forgot about Granny Hutch. When she remembered, she couldn't find her. Finally she saw her on the edge of the crowd. She's hunting for Jim Millican, Eve thought. Please, God, if you don't mind, don't let her find him. She might make him take me back.

At noon, a barbecued dinner was served across the creek. The big crowd of men, women, and children had to walk a couple of planks across the water to get to the table. It was made of planks laid in an L-shape, with one iron washpot of beans simmering in the center. Another iron washpot held the smoking coffee.

Eve liked skipping across the planks at the creek. The water gurgled beneath. The beef smelled good. The pickles and onions looked inviting. "I don't think I was ever so hungry," she told Granny Hutch.

They finished eating. Then Eve helped Granny Hutch gather up a tow sack of scraps to take home to the pig and the chickens. "Well," said Granny Hutch, "it's time to go as soon as you ride the hobby horse and buy that stick of striped peppermint. I've sold all the melons. We'll stop in Marty and you can pick out some flowerdy print for a dress."

They rode quietly after they left Marty. Eve had found a pretty print, brown with sprigs of pink roses in it. Now she was trying hard not to think about going back to the Home. Still, she'd just about run out of reasons to stay.

Granny Hutch slowed down long enough for an armadillo to lumber across the road. Then she said, "Eve, would you believe it? Old Bess is nigh onto twenty years old. She never had a colt. But she's been running up and down Dog Branch with John Devvies' stallion for some bit. Now she's in foal."

It was too bad there wasn't room on the pickup seat for Eve to dance. She was so excited that she asked what Granny Hutch declared was a million questions. She still was asking them when Granny Hutch stopped at the cabin. "I declare," Granny Hutch said, "you've got that glory look till your face looks like sunshine behind a rain cloud."

Eve did dance while they unloaded the pickup. She held the new broom in front of her for a partner. Suddenly, though, she stopped. The glory look went out of her face. "Granny Hutch," she cried, "I can't go back to the Home now. I just can't. I'd never know then what Old Bess's colt is like." She caught Granny Hutch's hand. "Please," she begged. "Pretty please."

Granny Hutch turned and began lifting provisions from the pickup bed. "Please, God," Eve whispered, "soften her heart. I just can't go now, God. I think you'll just have to do something."

Granny Hutch lifted out a sack of flour. "Well," she said finally, "I don't figure it'll be more than two months till the colt is born. Guess I could let you stay that long. Guess you could help me get in the winter wood." She handed Eve a bag of groceries. "But mind you," she warned, "you're not staying any longer."

Thank you, God, Eve said silently. You nearly let

her pull me across the line that time.

They hurried with the night work, for a big cloud was coming up fast. "That's a regular Texas thunderstorm," Granny Hutch declared. "When we started to the cowpen that cloud was barely peeking over the hills. No bigger than a bed blanket. Now it's covered the sky." She handed Eve the bucket of milk. "You go on to the cabin," she said. "I'll stop by for some cooking wood."

Granny Hutch lit the lamp when they were inside. Eve saw that her face looked drawn and worried. "Never thought I was a coward," she told Eve, "but I'm scared of clouds. I was in a cyclone one time. I can still see the wooden tower of the windmill going around the cabin like it was being carried out feet first." She began to undress. "Let's blow out the light and get to bed. I'm glad we ate coming from Marty."

They lay quietly in the darkness. Outside, the winds gathered. Then there was a calm. Eve whispered, "Can you hear it? That awful quiet?"

"I can. It's thick enough to cut with a butcher knife. Cover up your head. I've got mine covered."

"You ought to have a dog," Eve said.

"Don't know as a dog would help. They're fearful of clouds too. Now go to sleep."

A cricket complained now and then. The stillness went on. It crept closer and closer . . . waiting . . . Granny Hutch slept.

A flash of lightning zigzagged through the window. It woke Eve. Thunder ripped and rumbled overhead. Eve remembered what Granny Hutch told her. "When

I was little, I'd crawl under the bed when it thundered. Papa would drag me out. He'd say, 'Nothing to be scared of. That's God driving his potato wagon across the sky.'"

More lightning flashed. Again the thunder rolled. God sure must be driving his potato wagon fast, Eve thought. Another flash lit up the flat between the cabin and Dog Branch. It played across Granny Hutch's sleeping face. Eve got up quietly. I've got to see this, she thought. It beats last night's fireworks.

She wrapped a light quilt about her shoulders and stepped out on the stoop. She was careful that her bare feet made no sound. Granny Hutch was tired, and she was afraid. Eve didn't want to wake her. Lightning played across the yard and all the way to Dog Branch.

She ran swiftly so she wouldn't miss anything. She reached the Indian daisies and sat among them. Then she heard the lightning hit with a soft, sickening thud. I bet it hit the big pecan tree, Eve thought. Thank goodness, the baby cranes have flown. The bluish light brightened. It played over what had been the pecan tree. Now it was a pile of shattered wood. The tree had been split as neatly as John Devvies split Granny Hutch's cooking wood.

She was still sitting among the daisies when Granny Hutch found her. Granny Hutch pulled Eve to her feet. "Child," she shouted, "are you daft in the head?" She shook Eve soundly.

"I was watching God's show," Eve shouted against the gathering winds. "I just wish you could have seen it. God's really got the fireworks." She caught to

Granny Hutch to keep the wind from blowing her over. Then she laughed. "I bet last night when God saw the fireworks on the baseball ground he winked at his angels. 'We'll show them some real fireworks tomorrow night,' I bet he told them."

A big sprinkle of rain saved Granny Hutch from speaking her mind. They hurried through the wind-whipped daisies. They were sprinting toward the cabin when Eve asked, "Did you see how lightning split the big pecan? You've got a nice pile of cooking wood."

"Hush," Granny Hutch said sharply. They reached the cabin thoroughly wet. Granny Hutch hunted up dry sleeping garments. Then she said, "You've mighty nigh scared me out of my wits."

Eve was quiet as they went to bed. "Granny Hutch," she said finally, "I didn't mean to scare you."

"Well, land sakes, what did you mean?"

"It's just that when a storm came up at the Home, here would come the housemother. She'd draw every curtain. She'd make us listen while she read stories. And all the time the storm would be tearing itself out." Eve was quiet for a moment, then said, "That's why I just had to see this one."

Granny Hutch said, "Eve, there are some things a body has to be afraid of. Out here in these hills it takes a heap of fear to live. It takes a heap of looking out for yourself, too."

"I'll try," Eve said. "I'll try hard as I can. Surely I can learn how to be afraid. I've learned so many other things since I've been here." In the dark she began counting them off on her fingers. "I can hoe. I can build a fire. I can beat up corn batter. And now," she drew in a big deep breath, "now I've learned that Old Bess is going to have a colt."

Granny Hutch said, "And I've learned that you didn't use a bit of the sense the Lord gave you when you went out in that storm."

Eve yawned. She said softly, "I wonder if it really matters where we are. If lightning had struck the cabin, wouldn't it have been better if we'd both been sitting on Dog Branch?"

"Go to sleep," Granny Hutch said sharply. "You've gone and fouled up my thinking again."

7

July wore on. The cicadas sang more than they did in June. Eve found their shells split down the backs so they could crawl out easily. A nice way to get a new coat, she thought.

Granny Hutch talked less and less. It was as if she'd gone into another world. She's like the locusts, Eve thought. She has crawled away and just left her shell. She watched Granny Hutch come slowly out of the smokehouse. Her face was in the shade of her split bonnet. But Eve could see her eyes. They were dark and sad looking. I wish we could talk and laugh together, Eve thought. It would be fun.

However, there was Old Bess to talk to. Eve never rode the mare now. Old Bess was carrying her colt heavier each day. That was load enough.

One afternoon they walked past Cindy's grave. Eve had been telling the mare how Granny Hutch was there and yet she wasn't there. "Anyway," Eve told the mare, "she's stopped talking about sending me back to the Home."

Old Bess looked wise and twitched her ears.

They waded Dog Branch. "Now I'm in a spot," Eve

went on as they headed for the horse lot. "You see, I simply can't wait till your colt comes. Yet I simply can't stand to go back." She patted the mare's full sides. "Who knows, though. Something's likely to turn up the last minute so I can stay." She put her cheek against Old Bess. Together they walked on to the horse lot.

The first week in August Eve found the big rattlesnake. Wildflowers were everywhere, laughing at the drought. Granny Hutch couldn't keep Eve in the cabin.

"A house is to warm you or to hold you when you sleep," Eve told her. "But I don't need warming in August. So don't look for me. Not till it's time to do up the night work." She whirled on her bare toes. "Look at the world outside," she said. "It's just begging to be learned."

Up on the hillsides the Tiny Tims bloomed. Their thyme-like perfume smelled up the summer air. Against the old rock fence the Texas blazing star banked. Its long spikes bristled with lavender stars.

Granny Hutch didn't mind Eve's picking the Tiny Tims. They grew dwarf-clumped where vegetation was scanty and the ground easy to see. But she did mind Eve's prowling about the tumbled-down rock fence. "Someday," Eve said, coming in with an armful of the blazing star, "I'm going to count these little flowers. I bet there are a thousand stars on each spike."

"You stay away from that rock fence," Granny Hutch scolded. "Rattlesnakes love to coil up among cool rocks. But by August their skin starts getting so thick and scaly they go nearly blind. When they get so they can't see they get mad or afraid. Anyway, they're mighty touchy about it."

Eve laughed off her caution. "I'll be careful," she said, "but I can't stay inside." She held up a spray of the blazing star. "You know," she said, "I've been noticing something about wildflowers. The star is their favorite pattern. See, this spike is a good two feet long. And it's got one teensy lavender star after another. All around it. Now isn't that something?"

But Granny Hutch had gone too far off in her thoughts to answer.

Later Eve came in with an armload of purple eryngo. Her hands and arms were scratched from the stickery leaves. "Look what I found on the far side of the rock fence," she told Granny Hutch. "A whole patch of eryngo. Maybe you call it purple thistle. Anyway, it sure makes a pretty purple patch."

Granny Hutch stood the thistle in a brown crock. "Many's the time," she told Eve, "I've gathered it in the early fall and dried it for winter decoration. But I never called it such a name as eryngo."

Eve followed Granny Hutch out to the back yard where she was making soap. The bugs had begun to riddle the edges of the sidemeat out in the smokehouse. Eve and Granny Hutch had had to trim, slice, and then pack the remaining meat in stone jars of lard. Granny Hutch had used the trimmings to make lye soap.

She stirred the liquid in the black iron washpot. "There's something about making soap I always liked," she told Eve. "I like to see the strong lye eat the chunks of meat."

Eve watched the swirling black liquid. "I never saw anybody make soap before," she said. "I always just took soap for granted."

"Pour in a little more water," Granny Hutch went on, "then I poke up the fire. The water boils. The lye eats. I add more water, a little at a time."

"It must take lots of patience," Eve said.

"Sure does. That Viry can't make soap worth a hoot. No matter how long she stirs it the grease floats to the top. The lye sinks to the bottom. And that lye water is dark and skin-peeling strong. John Devvies says he reckons that Viry's too high-tempered to make soap."

She's talking, Eve thought happily. Granny Hutch is actually talking again. She had to keep her going. "Tell me more. I want to know all about it."

Granny Hutch went on stirring. "I always like to cut the soap when it's ready. I crisscross it. Then I lift out the first chunk with the butter paddle. After that they all slide out, easy like." A look of pain crossed her face. "I was making soap," she said, "when Cindy sickened."

Gently Eve took the soap paddle from her. She stirred the liquid until the swirl stood up like cake icing. Then she handed back the paddle. I wish I could put my arms about her, Eve thought. But I don't dare. Instead, she said, "I believe I'll take another walk. I'll be back in time to help with the night work."

She went by Granny Hutch and patted her arm. Granny Hutch stood there for a moment. Then she turned her back. Eve walked away.

Soon she came tearing back calling for Granny Hutch in an out-of-breath voice. "I saw the biggest rattlesnake," she cried. "He was down where I found the eryngo. He had a funny looking flat head and puffed-out jaws. He looked like maybe he'd chewed such a big bite he couldn't swallow." She stopped for breath while Granny Hutch whirled to face her. "We just looked at each other," Eve went on. "He was the first rattlesnake I'd ever seen. Maybe I was the first girl he'd ever seen. Anyway, he was beautiful."

Granny Hutch caught Eve by her shoulders. "I told you to stay away from that rock fence," she shouted. She shook Eve. "So that rattlesnake was beautiful, was he? Well, let me tell you if that rattlesnake had bitten you this far from a doctor, chances are nothing on God's earth could have saved you. You don't bring a rattlesnake to the house like you would a bunch of flowers. A rattlesnake's a deadly thing. Animals have enough sense to know it. I just wish you did."

She shook Eve again. "If you couldn't kill him, at least, you could have hit him with a rock and broken his back so he couldn't coil. Then I could have come and finished him."

Eve's eyes held tears. "I didn't want to kill him," she said slowly. "He wants to live the same as I do." She smiled at Granny Hutch through her tears. "He didn't even rattle to scare me. He looked so nice I named him Mr. Captain."

"The sun's too low to hunt him now," Granny Hutch said. "But we've got to find him." She covered the soap with a folded tarp and turned to Eve.

"Child," she said sternly, "you've got to come out of your glory world long enough to listen to me. You've never seen somebody bitten by a rattlesnake. If it's leg or arm, either swells the size of my butter churn." Eve paled, but Granny Hutch went on. "If that snake bites with his fangs full of poison, it takes a heap of luck to save whoever or whatever is bitten."

Eve said, "I've read the Tejas Indians had a sure cure for rattlesnake bite, but they wouldn't give their cure to the white man."

"Well, if things go right, the white man knows a trick or two. If it happens close to a chicken pen, they just grab up a chicken and split it down the back. Then they slap it on the bite. When it turns green from the poison, they catch up another. Or maybe the bite can be slashed open and the poison sucked out by mouth." Again she looked sternly at Eve. "If things aren't handy, folks die."

Eve sat down suddenly. Presently she said, "If I didn't bother Mr. Captain he wouldn't have bothered me, would he? Of course, if he'd chased me and tried to bite me, I would have had to defend myself. But he didn't chase me. He just coiled nicely and looked at me."

"He coiled so he could strike. A rattlesnake doesn't go chasing folks like a mad bull. A rattlesnake coils and uncoils quicker than you can even watch. He has to coil so he can jump his length. And it's not often he misjudges how far he can strike." Granny Hutch studied Eve's pasty face. "The good Lord didn't put rattlesnakes here to be played with like toys." She turned away angrily. "Mr. Captain, my foot! I'll be glad when you go back to the Home. Mighty glad."

Suddenly Eve could stand no more. She ran in the direction of the willow. The late sun was in her eyes. She didn't see John Devvies walking down the road until she ran against him.

"Hold it, Glory Girl. You having running fits? My Liver Pill gets 'em when he's wormy." Gently John Devvies took Eve by the shoulders. "Why, bless me, where's the glory look? My, my, I do believe she's crying."

He led Eve to a gap in the rock fence. He lifted her and sat her on the top rock. Then he climbed up and sat beside her. The four hounds came up and lay at their feet like dead. John Devvies took a red bandanna from his pocket. He wiped Eve's eyes. "Now," he said, "we'll just sit a spell till things straighten out."

Eve told him the whole story. John Devvies sat, whistling through his teeth. Presently he said, "So Granny Hutch bawled you out, did she?"

"She shook me," Eve sobbed. "She said she'd be glad when I went back."

"Now, now, we're not going to let you go back." Again he wiped Eve's eyes. "This ole handky's getting mighty wet," he decided. "May have to wring it out and dry it on that catclaw yonder." He went on whistling through his teeth.

Liver Pill opened one eye. He looked at Eve with such a wealth of sorrow that she had to laugh.

"Now," said John Devvies, "that's better." He took off his red cap and stashed it in its accustomed place under his left arm. "It's been a year," he went on, "a year this week since Cindy died. Now I figure Granny Hutch might not be sleeping any too well these nights. Reckon you're too young to know these things. A body has to go the road before he knows the way."

From the willow a mockingbird broke out in a wild song. John Devvies said, "Take my Viry. Four babies Viry's had. Not one of them lived. Only one, little Ellie, ever breathed. And in that four hours Ellie lived I planned a whole lifetime of fun for her and me. She'd be about your age now."

They heard Granny Hutch calling from the kitchen window. John Devvies grinned and stood up. "I'll fix her," he said. He put back his head and let out his Rebel yell. The hills caught up his voice and threw it along the ridges and through the trees. "He, he, he," John Devvies chuckled. "Bet she jumped two feet in the air when she heard that."

Just the thoughts of Granny Hutch's jumping two feet in the air made Eve laugh. "Now," said John Devvies, "that's better." He lifted Eve off the fence. "Let's get going," he said. "I gotta stop by Granny Hutch's long enough to give her this deer ham. Then I gotta stay long enough for her to give me fits. Then I gotta go on home. Figure Viry'll have to finish her tongue lashing before she sets out supper."

8

September came. The days were hotter even that
those in August. But the nights were cool and good for
sleeping. The colt hadn't been born yet. Eve was glad.
I'm dying to see it, she thought. Simply dying to see it.
But as long as it's not here Granny Hutch won't send
me back.

"She was careful not to mention the promise. Maybe by the time the colt is born, she kept reminding
herself, something else will come up. Maybe I'll be so
much help by then that Granny Hutch will find me—
now what was that word Miss Woodruff used to show
how the plants needed light? Indispensable. Eve
giggled, just picturing Granny Hutch's face if she used
such a word in front of her.

In the afternoons, after the morning dews had
dried, she helped Granny Hutch pick the whipporwill
peas. Their pods were white-dried now, with no sign of
their purpled-specked green. They threshed the peas on
a wagon sheet along the banks of Dog Branch. The first
windy day they fanned the chaff out of them. "Oh, I
love winnowing peas," Eve said happily.

"Well," Granny Hutch said tiredly, "I thought we

were fanning the peas. I never heard of a body winnowing them.''

They poured the clean peas into jars. "Now I'll get
the highlife," Granny Hutch said. "That keeps the wee-
vils out.''

They'd barely finished when John Devvies drove
up in a frenzy. "Gonna start making molasses tomorrow,'' he yelled before he got his truck stopped.
"Better be there with your cane bright and early.''

"Watch your hounds," Granny Hutch yelled as all
four dogs jumped out of the pickup bed and ran to
sniff the jars of peas. "Let them turn over one jar,
John Devvies, just one jar. They'll wish they hadn't.''

"Get on home," John Devvies ordered his dogs.
The hounds made a beeline for the truck. They
scooted under it and lay there like dead. "Or under the
truck, one." He jumped out and came over to Eve. "So
you're here," he said. He put on a big show of lowering
his voice. "I knew all the time she didn't aim to send
you back.''

Granny Hutch glared at him. "I'm aiming to send
Eve back," she declared, "and I don't need any prying
neighbor to remind me.''

John Devvies tweaked one of Eve's plaits and
chuckled. "He, he, he. Got Granny riled that time," he
said. He sobered and brought a spool of white thread
out of his pocket. "Found this little bitty spool of
sewing thread right in the middle of Dog Branch," he
told Granny Hutch. "Thought maybe you'd be needing
to sew some clothes for Glory Girl.''

Granny Hutch had to smile. She took the thread.

"John Devvies," she said, "I've been living on Dog Branch for many a year. I've never found a spool of thread in it." She tucked the spool inside the pocket of her dress. "Might as well take it," she told John Devvies. "You'd leave it if you had to tie it around a jar of peas."

"It's for Glory Girl," John Devvies said. "You be needing that little old girl mighty bad. I aim to do my best to see that you keep her."

"John Devvies, I don't need anybody. I've always looked after myself. I still can."

"Aw, you need that girl. You need her bad." He headed for his pickup.

"We'll have a load of cane there by first bird call," Granny Hutch yelled after him. "And you be tending your own business. I'll tend to mine."

John Devvies chuckled happily. He turned his pickup around and tore off down the road.

"Never in my life did I see such a fizzling man," Granny Hutch grumbled. "Why couldn't he have told me a day earlier that he'd be making molasses. I'd have had time then to get ready." She looked at Eve. "Reckon you're going to learn what goes on before a body pours molasses out of a pitcher," she said.

"Oh, I'll love learning how," Eve said. "It will be one more lesson I've learned since I've been here."

They hurried with the peas to the smokehouse. Then they went around to the back where Granny Hutch picked up some stout paddles from under a shed. "I stored these planks here last year," she told Eve. "I keep them for stripping the leaves off the cane."

Eve helped her carry the boards to the cane field, which joined the melon patch. "Take one board, like this," Granny Hutch showed Eve. "Turn it so and slash the blades from the cane stalks."

"Like this?" Eve made an awkward slash.

"No. Hold your plank this way. And mind you stay clear of those cane blades. They're keen-edged as a butcher knife. They'll cut your arms like a razor."

She handed Eve another plank. "When you've stripped leaves till your board's wet," she said, "lay it down to dry. Then pick up another."

Soon Eve caught on. She began slashing in high glee. "I'm playing like I'm scalping Indians," she told Granny Hutch.

Granny Hutch shook her head. "I declare," she said, "I never know from one minute to the next what kind of an idea lives in your head."

They worked hard. When they had finished with the blades, they cut the heads from the stalks. "I guess Old Bess is through eating by now," Granny Hutch said. "We'll go let her out of the horse lot and bring back the pickup."

Soon they were back in the field. Granny Hutch said, "I'm right proud of my cane heads. They'll make many a feed for Old Rose and the chickens and the shoat."

"Yes," Eve said. "And I just bet Old Bess would eat them if she ran out of corn."

They loaded fast. Steam rose from the ground about them. It mingled with the steam from the green cane. I'll never forget this good smell, Eve thought as she worked.

Granny Hutch grumbled. "Drat that John Devvies. He could have told us yesterday."

"Never mind," Eve said. "We'll be started in the morning by first bird call." I've never heard that expression before, she thought. It sounds a little like poetry.

The next morning at daylight Eve and Granny Hutch drove up to the John Devvies mill. Eve rode behind on the load of cane. She'd taken along Granny Hutch's short butcher knife. Now she peeled one joint after another, chewing the juice and spitting out the pith.

Granny Hutch drove her pickup on down closer to the mill. "I'm mighty glad to be here," she said, "another mile of raw cane juice and you'd be doubling over with the colic."

Eve jumped down from the load of cane. Granny Hutch looked her over and frowned. "I wanted you to look all spic and span when we got here," she sighed. "Viry's so snooty. Now you're all mussed up."

Eve laughed. "I don't give a hootenany what Viry thinks. I'm having fun."

"Where did you learn that hootenany?" Granny Hutch said sharply.

"Oh," Eve said airily, "I borrowed it from Mr. Devvies."

John Devvies was already at his mill. He'd built it at the end of the cane rows. Eve looked at his fields stripped of stubble. She said to Granny Hutch, "The pastures of postoak, blackjack, and wild china look like an autumn frame around the cane field."

Granny Hutch looked. "Why, so it does. But I never looked at a pasture of trees before and thought they made a picture frame."

John Devvies motioned for them to unload on the rack. Then he cranked his gasoline-powered engine and fed cane into the press. He moved slowly, walking in a circle as the press turned, squeezing out the juice. "He's not like that when he drives his pickup to Marty," Eve said.

"John Devvies is a master hand at molasses making," Granny Hutch said. "He's not running from Viry now, nor sounding off any Rebel yell."

"Gee-haw—hoo-up!" John Devvies' voice was soft. He fed the stalks into the mill. They spewed out, flattened, from a slot on the other side. He siphoned off the juice to the vats resting on the open-faced furnace. There Viry, decked out again like a flowered tent, stirred and tasted. She never once looked in the direction of Eve and Granny Hutch. "Guess we're still poor white trash," Eve whispered. Granny Hutch shook her head. She didn't want Viry aroused.

Eve went to where Viry was stirring. "I never knew before," she said to Viry's upturned nose, "that it took all this to make molasses."

Viry's sniff was like a gander's hiss. She turned her back to Eve and kept stirring. Eve didn't notice. She watched the bubbling, foam-flecked juice thicken. She saw it turn to muddy brown water. Viry plunged her gourd dipper into the seething mass. The liquid became dark red molasses. Why, this is creation, Eve thought in wonder. I've just seen something turn into something else.

71

John Devvies came over. He took the gourd dipper from Viry. He bent over and dipped up some of the juice. "Drink this," he said to Eve. "Mind you cool it before sticking a tongue to it." He pretended he didn't even see Viry's frown.

Eve took the dipper and blew little waves on the juice. She didn't notice how Viry's hands found her well-larded hips. She didn't notice how Viry glared at John Devvies. She sipped. Then she lowered her head and drank. "That child will be sick," Viry muttered to John Devvies. "You watch what I tell you."

John Devvies winked at Eve and went back to the fire.

"John Devvies is an expert at firing the vats," Granny Hutch said. "He knows right when it's time to build up or to lower the fire. That way, the juice can simmer at the right heat."

Even when they started back for the second load of cane Eve still was wondering about it all. "It's something," she said, "to watch that juice foam and rush down the flume." She hugged her knees as she sat by Granny Hutch on the seat. "I guess it's a flume. Anyway, it's whatever that trough running from the mill is called. And when the juice trickles into the vats, the way it seethes and simmers you'd think it was alive."

Granny Hutch turned the pickup around a mesquite stump. "Well," she said, "I've seen molasses made all my life. All it looks like to me is a sight of hard work."

"Oh," said Eve, "did you ever really watch it whenever it's stirred and then skimmed? It turns from a frothy green to exactly the color of Mr. Devvies' mules." She caught her breath, then added, "Mr. Devvies let me spoon the skimming from the vat that had done cooking. He showed me how to hold up the spoon to the air and lick it like candy. Talk about ambrosia." Eve shut her eyes, just remembering.

"And did he show you how to double up with the colic? My land, if you don't get sick I'll never figure out why."

Eve was quiet until they reached the cane patch. Finally she said, "Funny, but with all their education I bet not a teacher at the Home knows how to make molasses."

Granny Hutch smiled as she stopped the pickup. "Do you know how?" she asked.

"Do I know how to make molasses?" Eve was shocked. "I watched till I learned it all. From beginning to end. Alpha to omega."

"My," Granny Hutch said, "you do say the strangest words. They're right pretty, though."

Eve hopped out and began loading cane. "It's a lesson I could never forget," she said solemnly.

"Not even if you get the stomachache?"

"Not even if I get the stomachache."

The sun was tilting westward by the time they loaded and started. They didn't even dare to stop by the cabin. They had to reach the mill and get back by night.

Presently Granny Hutch fumbled around under the seat and came up with a basket of cornbread, bacon, and a jug of buttermilk. "I knew better than to depend on Viry to ask us to eat," she said.

"We could have done without," Eve told her. "I'm already full of cane juice and molasses anyway."

"My land," Granny Hutch said after she'd poured Eve a third mug of buttermilk, "what went with all that cane juice?"

Eve's eyes danced. "That juice was just an appetizer," she said. "This is the real meal." Over the mug her eyes smiled at Granny Hutch. "And the best meal I ever ate."

John Devvies laid his stirring paddle carefully on the rim of the vat when they drove up. "I whittled you a little present while you were gone," he told Eve. From his hip pocket he took out a doll. It was crudely carved from the red-brown wood of a mesquite.

Tenderly Eve took the little doll. There were tears in her eyes when she turned to thank John Devvies. "I never had somebody make a present just for me," she said.

"Shucks now," John Devvies was embarrassed. "I never figured a little bitty doll would make you cry. Reckon I'll just have to take it back."

"Oh, no you don't." Through her tears Eve was laughing now.

John Devvies watched her cradle the little doll in her arms. "Now," he said, "that smile looks better. Why, bless me you got that glory look clean over your whole face."

Viry sniffed a sniff that wound up a snort. She sailed into John Devvies for piddling away his time.

When they started home, Granny Hutch drove a bit

74

faster than she wanted to. They barely had time to store the crocks of warm molasses inside the smoke-house before a moonless but starry night shut them in.

They'd turned the calf with Old Rose in case they couldn't get home to milk. Now by lantern light they felt their way to the cowlot to separate them. The shoat grunted inside his pen. To Eve he smelled of black mud and night air. "He's hungry," Granny Hutch said. "But recollecting your Mr. Captain, I wouldn't be caught putting my hand inside that corncrib. I'll throw him this apron full of cane heads I aimed to feed the chickens. I reckon he'll make out till morning."

Inside the cabin Eve lit the lamp. The glory look was still on her face. "I've never had a happier day," she said as she laid the little wooden doll on her pillow.

She undressed and lay down beside the doll. She thought how kind Granny Hutch had been all day. Maybe she'll decide to keep me after all, Eve thought. She rolled over and doubled up her knees. "Goodnight, God," she whispered, "and thank you."

Granny Hutch lay down tiredly. "I reckon I'm lucky having all that molasses," she said, "so I guess it's been a good day for me, too."

The night wasn't so good. Granny Hutch had one leg cramp after another. Eve couldn't sleep. She lay there listening to the wind fussing and calling outside. She pictured winter mornings with sourdough biscuits baked in the Dutch oven. She could see them buttered, then molasses poured over them. For some reason, though, the molasses didn't make such a good picture.

Toward morning she got up, went to the door, and vomited cane juice.

Her forehead felt feverish. Granny Hutch was glad when the dominecker rooster crowed for day. Eve couldn't eat any gruel for breakfast so Granny Hutch brought her a little strong coffee. It was smoking hot. Eve sipped it and said, "There's one word I sure don't want you to say today."

"Well," said Granny Hutch, "I can't rightly figure out what word you mean."

"Think, Granny Hutch. Think."

"Is it Viry?"

"Nope," said Eve, "it's molass--." She barely made it to the hearth before the coffee came up.

Granny Hutch held her head at the hearth. She wiped her face with a wet cloth. "Sit still," she told Eve. "I'll go in and plump up your pillow."

"Wait a minute," Eve cried, jumping up. She was too weak, though, so she sat down again. I hope she'll see it and be careful with it, she thought. For in the hollow of her pillow Eve had laid the little wooden doll.

9

The colt was born in October. Eve and Granny Hutch found it in the neck of the far field. There the tansy asters purpled the postoak woodland. They had missed Old Bess that morning when they went to the cow lot. Eve threw the shoat a lapful of corn nubbins. She turned to Granny Hutch with shining eyes. "I bet it's happened," she said.

Granny Hutch got off the milking stool to back Old Rose's hind foot. "It always did vex me," she grumbled, "to milk a cow with her hind leg between me and the milk. Back your foot," she ordered Old Rose. Her hand pushed hard against the cow's hip. Old Rose backed so fast she struck the bucket of milk. Half of it spilled.

Eve laughed merrily as she came through the gate. "Don't look so glum," she told Granny Hutch. "This day is too special to fret over spilled milk. I'll drink one cup less for supper."

She skipped beside Granny Hutch as they carried the milk to the cabin. They washed, and Eve ran to the back yard fence for the cloth through which Granny Hutch strained the milk. "Hurry," she begged. Her feet were fairly dancing. "Let's go find them."

They walked to where Granny Hutch's land joined that of John Devvies. They turned down Dog Branch to the neck of the far field, where they found the mare and colt.

Old Bess stood patiently. Her dappled sides were relieved now of their load. Her black udder dripped milk as her colt mouthed hungrily.

Eve was on her knees now, fondling the colt's silky flanks. "Look at him," she cried. "He's standing knee deep in tansy asters. He's so pretty, all brown against their purple."

Granny Hutch tried to hide her own excitement. "My, my," she said. "John Devvies ought to be here to see that glory look all over your face."

Eve jumped up and caught the colt's head between her hands. "He's got a star on his forehead," she cried. "It's a white star, and it's perfect. Nope, that point looking at his right eye is a mite longer."

Granny Hutch came up to the colt. "The way you're hopping around I'm reminded of my old domi-necker rooster chasing a grasshopper."

Eve didn't hear a word. "We'll name him Tansy," she said to Granny Hutch. "See, he was born in the tansy asters."

"Well," Granny Hutch said, "seeing he's all brown, I'd figured to name him John Brown." She saw Eve's face and added, "But I reckon he'll grow just as fast named Tansy."

Eve rubbed Tansy's back. She said, "That's the way Mr. Devvies named his little mules. One is called

Sugar Cane because he was born in the cane patch. The other is named Sandstorm. Mr. Devvies said he was born in a real Texas sandstorm."

"Tansy's all right for a name," Granny Hutch said. "I'm too thankful that Old Bess is fine to argue." She clapped her hands and clacked her tongue to the mare. "We'd best start home," she said. "The colt's too wobbly-legged to travel fast. Besides, Old Bess needs a good feed of yellow corn. She's had quite a night."

They had plenty of time to look the colt over as they moved along home. "He's a good one," Granny Hutch decided. "His head is well shaped. He's broad between the eyes, and his hindquarters show plenty of driving and pulling power."

"He ought to be fine," Eve said. "Old Bess is tops, and Mr. Devvies' stallion is a fine horse, too."

"That colt ought to make a powerful horse," Granny Hutch declared.

"What breed would you call Tansy?" Eve wanted to know.

"Well, he's Percheron from Old Bess and the stallion's father was out of the Steel Dust strain."

"Steel Dust? Whatever is Steel Dust?"

They had come to a spreading postoak. Granny Hutch said, "We'll sit in the shade and rest the colt a spell." They stopped Old Bess. "Steel Dust," Granny Hutch explained, "was a fine stallion brought from Kentucky to Texas. Before Hill folk got so poor after the Civil War, cattlemen bred their mares to him. His owner stood him somewheres around Dallas."

"A long way to go," Eve said. Her eyes were on Tansy.

"John Devvies' great-grandfather bred his mare to Steel Dust. Tansy's father is out of her strain."

All about them the leaves were changing color. The postoaks were taking on a russet brown. The black-jacks promised within a month to be a rosy red. Up in the near hills a few sumac bushes were already flaming scarlet. Eve looked up at the sky. It's the color of bluebells, she thought. Tansy snored.

Eve watched the colt and shook with silent laughter. Now and then he'd twitch an ear in her direction. "He hears me laughing inside," she whispered to Granny Hutch.

Granny Hutch rubbed her tired legs. "I forgot to tell you," she said, "that colt's got racing blood. Steel Dust was a famous race horse."

The sun was already slanting toward the western hills by the time they got the mare and colt in the horse lot. "I reckon we'll have to call this meal dinner and supper," Granny Hutch said as they sat down to eat.

But Eve didn't hear. She chewed her food but she didn't know what she ate. Her world held nothing now except a brown, high-legged colt called Tansy.

About dark John Devvies drove over to borrow some kerosene oil for his lantern. "Been aiming to head for Marty and get some oil," he said. "Just been waiting around for Viry to make me mad enough to go."

He jumped up and began prowling the kitchen. All

four hounds were at his heels. Eve brought the kerosene and set it under the kitchen table where maybe the dogs wouldn't turn it over. Presently John Devvies turned and glared at Granny Hutch. "Know what Viry's got in her mind to do?" he asked. "She's aiming for me to pipe water to the house."

"Maybe she wants handy water," Granny Hutch said.

"Why, we got water in Dog Branch. That ought to be good enough for Viry. But no. She's got to putting on airs. Wants her water in the house. Aims for me to break my back with all that digging." He broke off as Eve came back into the kitchen with a lighted lantern. "Where you going with that lantern?" he wanted to know.

Eve tugged at his sleeve. "Come with me to the horse lot," she begged. "I've got something to show you."

They were gone for some time. When they came back Eve was arguing. John Devvies was laughing. He shooed the dogs under Granny Hutch's bed. "I'll be back for my colt in about three, four weeks," he said. His blue eyes danced as he gave Granny Hutch a slow wink.

Eve caught the joke. "How come the colt is yours?" she wanted to know.

"He's the spitting image of my stallion. Reckon my horse just can't deny his son."

"But what about Old Bess? She foaled him."

"Pshaw now, that's a minor detail. Just a little old minor detail."

Granny Hutch said, "I hate to break up the argument but when you go to Marty I wish you'd stop by. I think I might be able to rake up enough money to send Eve with you. She can catch a Greyhound bus back to the Home."

Anger wiped out the fun in John Devvies' eyes. "Now look what you've gone and done," he cried. "You've clean wiped all the glory from that child's face. Just because you're too stubborn to say you need her. Shame on you!"

Granny Hutch whirled on him. "Do you think I like making Eve unhappy?" she asked. "John Devvies, I'm an old woman. I've got nothing to offer that child. Right now, I don't have too much gasoline in the pickup and if I fill it up when the gas truck comes by then I won't have the money to send Eve back on the bus. She's got to leave soon or it's going to be mighty hard for her to leave that colt."

Angrily John Devvies shooed his dogs out from under the bed and opened the kitchen door for them. He turned back and looked at Granny Hutch. Eve had never seen anger in his eyes before. "I left you a side of bacon in the smokehouse," he said.

He slammed the door hard behind him, then he flung it wide open. "I aim for Glory Girl to help you eat that bacon. When I go to Marty, I'll take the short cut through the pasture. I'm not about to take Glory Girl to the bus."

They sat quietly after John Devvies left. I ought to go, Eve thought. I just ought to get up and walk all the way from here to Marty. Still, I can't help but believe that Granny Hutch cares for me. She's afraid because she's poor and she's old. Aloud she said, "Mr. Devvies forgot his lamp oil. I could ride Old Bess over there tomorrow and take it to him."

Granny Hutch's face looked old and drawn. All her determination seemed to have left her. "Yes," she said absently, "you'd best take it over tomorrow."

The next morning was cold. A wind, raw and gusty for October, came out of the east. It showered down a clatter of acorns from the postoak. As soon as Eve had the fire going, she snatched up a shawl and ran to the horse lot.

Tansy was getting an early breakfast. Old Bess nosed him lovingly. "You don't have to ask me what I think of him," Eve told the big mare. "You've really birthed a fine colt." Gently she touched the crease in each of Tansy's hind legs. "Tansy," she teased, "you're a big old sissy. You've got dimples in your hind legs."

When she got back to the cabin she came over to the fire to warm her backside. "Bet you don't know where I've been," she told Granny Hutch.

Granny Hutch dipped breakfast mush from the dinner pot. "You don't need to say it in words," she answered. "Your face tells it all."

"Tansy knew me," Eve said. She opened the kitchen door to dash out the washpan water. "I just know he did."

"Well," said Granny Hutch, "sit down and eat your breakfast. With the wind gathering around towards the north, we'd best wash before it gets any colder."

Eve looked hungrily at the plate of sizzling hoecakes. Granny Hutch bowed her head. "Oh, Lord, bless this food given to the nourishment of our bodies."

"And thank you for Tansy," Eve added. She looked at Granny Hutch as she poured cream over her mush. "And thank you, Granny Hutch," she whispered to herself. "Thank you for not bringing up the subject of going back. I couldn't bear to listen to it this glorious morning. I couldn't. I couldn't. I couldn't."

10

That night they fed the cow and calf and shut the chickens in the hen house. With Old Bess and Tansy safe in the horse lot, they went to bed early.

They lay quietly, but they could not sleep. Finally Granny Hutch said, "I reckon your thoughts are like mine. They keep chasing each other like a pack of hounds trailing a deer by day then keeping at it all night."

Eve rolled over on her cot. "I guess maybe we're too excited over Tansy," she said.

"Could be. I thought when we got him to the horse lot we'd be over it. I reckon, though, it gets worse."

The moon filtered through the bedroom curtain. Granny Hutch said, "I used to sing to Cindy when we couldn't go to sleep. There was one song she loved in particular. It's called 'Froggy Went a Courtin'. I learned it the way the darkies sang it when I was a little girl. They had a funny chorus. Don't know where they got it."

Eve jumped up in the middle of her cot. She hugged her knees under her chin. "Sing it. Please do."

Granny Hutch began to sing:

"Froggie went a courtin', he did ride,
Latta-Bota-Rincktum-Kime-O;
Sword and pistol at his side,
Latta-Bota-Rincktum-Kime-O.
Come a nearo, Mel an Karo,
Come a Nearo Kime o,
Semi Nickel Bobba Nickel, Latta-Bota-Rincktum,
Rincktum, Rincktum, Latta-Bota-Rincktum-
Kime-O.

When she got to "He rode up to Miss Mouse's
house," Eve joined her. But she had trouble at first
with the Latta-Bota-Rincktums. Finally, though, she
learned them and joined in happily:
"He said, 'Miss Mouse, will you marry me?'
Latta-Bota-Rincktum-Kime-O."
They followed the whole romance to the descrip-
tion of the wedding guests. Eve laughed merrily when
they came to:
"Next guest in was a gentleman flea,
Latta-Bota-Rincktum-Kime-O;
With his banjo on his knee,
Latta-Bota-Rincktum-Kime-O."
By the time they'd finished with the wedding
supper and dance, Eve was quiet. Finally she said, "I
wonder why white folks can't put into a song what
colored folks can?"

"I don't know. Could be, the Negro knew to put all the color and music into words he could roll off his tongue easy like."

A cricket chirruped in the chimney corner. It waited, then got answered. The wind shifted, bringing in the smell of Dog Branch. The smell was dank and cold. Eve lay there, warm and light feeling. Through tightly shut eyes she was seeing the mare's tail weeds along Dog Branch. Their white-flowered limbs were gray now from long blooming, like Old Bess's tail. She declared to Granny Hutch the next morning that when she finally went to sleep she dreamed that fairies were dancing under them.

The next day Eve took the dollar Jim Millican had given her from under the cot mattress. She said to Granny Hutch, "I have to go see Mr. Devvies this morning. It's something about Christmas."

Granny Hutch sighed. She said, "I wish you wouldn't talk about Christmas. But if you're going, I think you'd better ride Old Bess. It's quite a ways to walk."

"Oh, I don't mind it. It's such a pretty sunshiny day."

Eve skipped out the kitchen door. She was glad she got away before Granny Hutch made her put on a bonnet.

The autumn leaves had finally turned. Now they were beautiful. "They'll look like that about a week," Granny Hutch said. "Then they'll get dull and start falling."

Eve stopped and looked around her. The pastures

were crimson and gold. The leaves of the postoaks were yellow-brown. The blackjack oaks were a rosy wine. Against the hills the sumac flamed like a red sunset. Then there were the green leaves of the liveoaks which did not shed in the winter. Eve could not look long enough. Miss Woodruff had said the autumn colors were caused by lack of chlorophyll, which went down in the fall. "I don't like to think it's just the trees without their usual chlorophyll," Eve said aloud. Her eyes were shining. "I like to think that Somebody moves among them when autumn comes and touches them and turns them to beautiful colors."

A cold nose touched her hand. It was Liver Pill. Eve hadn't seen John Devvies and his hounds. She hadn't seen anything but the autumn trees. "Well," said John Devvies, "who's the Somebody that touches these trees and turns them so pretty?"

"God," Eve said. "No human could do that."

John Devvies looked at Eve's face. Slowly his old red cap went under his left arm. "You've got that glory look on your face again," he said.

"And why shouldn't I?" Eve said happily. "Look all around you, Mr. Devvies. It's a Glory World."

Then she remembered. "I was coming to see you," she said. "I knew you wouldn't come by when you went to Marty." She handed him the dollar. "When you go to Marty," she told him, "I want you to buy Granny Hutch a pretty shawl for Christmas."

John Devvies took the dollar. "Shopping a bit early. Nope, I won't be coming by Granny Hutch's.

She aims to send you to Marty with me, and I don't aim to take you."

He grinned at Eve. "I sure miss coming by and seeing you and Granny Hutch," he said. He pocketed the dollar. "I'll buy her a shawl that'll knock her eyes out. Just you go down to the forks of the road next week. You'll find a package tied inside that bluethorn bush."

11

Before they knew it, November had come. The first V of wild geese flew over Dog Branch, honking southward.

"We'll haul the winter wood," Granny Hutch said. "Then I'll find something to make you a coat and a dress."

"I don't need much," Eve said happily. "Just something to keep me warm."

"Eve," Granny Hutch said firmly, "it's time I put you on the bus at Marty. You need to go before the new year comes."

Eve's face lost its happiness. She said, "It's been so long since you mentioned it. I hoped that you'd keep me."

"I've never said one time I'd keep you. I've been thinking John Devvies might forget and come by."

"He really is going to Marty by the short cut," Eve said.

"I figure he is. That man aims for me to keep you even if both of us starve. But it's wrong. You need education. Sure, I can send you on the school bus to

Marty but I'm not sure I can afford to keep you in school."

Eve came up to Granny Hutch. Her eyes were big with unshed tears. "If you won't take me for your grandchild," she said, "at least you could wait till the truant officer finds me. I wrote Miss Woodruff that I was somewhere in the Hill Country." She laughed a little. "I just hope the Marty postmark got blurred."

"We'll do up the winter work," Granny Hutch said. "Then I'll make your clothes. I could write the Home and tell the truant officer to come. But I don't want to be beholden to the Home. We'll let it go for a while."

"And you won't say any more about it?"

"I'll try not to. But if something comes up, I'll have your clothes ready."

"Maybe nothing will turn up," Eve said, happy again.

It was time to pull the turnips and store them. The sweet potatoes had to be dug before frost. Along Dog Branch the pecans had begun to fall. Wild asters flowered pink on the roadsides. The winter wood had to be hauled.

They hitched Old Bess to the buckboard. Pasture stumps might ruin the truck tires. With Tansy running and cutting capers, they hauled plenty of wood. Eve learned to use an axe. The maul and wedges, however, were too much for her.

With a practiced hand Granny Hutch tamped the three wedges along the grain of a big log. She picked up the maul.

"That maul is too heavy for you," Eve said. "I

could ride Old Bess over to Mr. Devvies. He'd split the logs."

"And have Viry come down with a conniption fit. No, thank you." Granny Hutch swung the ten-pound maul against the first wedge. She pulled it out and moved on down the log. Soon the log lay neatly cleft. Together she and Eve sawed the halves into fireplace wood.

"I still say it's too heavy for you," Eve worried.

"Shoo now. Just you watch how I split this stump." Granny Hutch tamped in the wedge. She swung the maul. The stump sliced to the ground. Eve swung the back of the axe against it. Now it was ready to load.

No matter how hard she worked, Eve still had time to run with Tansy. The two of them would tear off down the road. The colt's tail and Eve's plaits would be streaming out behind. "I declare," Granny Hutch said to Eve, "I can't figure whether the colt's turned human or you've turned colt."

They had a language all their own, Eve and Tansy. And Tansy would fairly dance whenever he saw Eve open the yard gate.

"Granny Hutch," Eve said one day, "look at Tansy's eyes. They're exactly the color of water after leaves fall in. I just can't wait to ride him." She ran her hands along the colt's cushioned back. "Next year I'm going to climb on his back. Then we're going to outrun the wind."

"Eve," Granny Hutch said sharply, "now you've gone and made me say it. Next year you'll be back at the Home."

When they'd finished hauling wood they dug the sweet potatoes. They cut the vines first to feed to Old Rose. Next they mounded the dug potatoes and turnips together. In the center they stood cornstalks upright. They left an airhole at the top and covered the stalks with gunny sacks. When they'd finished mounding up dirt all around, Eve stood back. She began to laugh. "It looks for all the world like Sitting Bull's teepee," she said.

The first real frost came that night. All up and down Dog Branch the next day there was the acid smell of green things dying.

Hog butchering was the worst job. They'd fattened the shoat by feeding him slop and milk and corn nubbins. By the third week in November Granny Hutch reckoned the shoat would weigh three hundred pounds on foot.

That morning they went out to tend everything. They found the shoat bedded down in a trough of leaves with just his snout and beady eyes showing. "Well," Granny Hutch said, "that shoat tells me it's butchering time."

"But I didn't hear him say anything, Granny Hutch."

Granny Hutch smiled. "You're always telling me that animals talk. When a shoat makes a bed of leaves, it means one of two things. Either that shoat's about to find pigs or a big norther's brewing. Now this shoat isn't a sow. So I don't figure he's telling me he's finding pigs."

Eve thought it was funny. But when she started to

pour slop into the shoat's trough, Granny Hutch stopped her. "Don't feed a hog about to be butchered," she said. "Just makes a messy job messier."

Under her freckles Eve's face went white. It was the first time she'd connected *butchering* the shoat with *killing* the shoat... She said, "Couldn't we get Mr. Devvies to do the butchering?"

"No," said Granny Hutch. "Viry would be mad, and John Devvies would tell me to fatten the shoat for more lard. I don't like fat meat. So we'll just fill the washpot and get the fire going. Then you can stay in the cabin while I shoot the shoat."

Eve's face was still white. She said, "I'll be eating the meat same as you. I won't run off."

They brought the water from Dog Branch. After it heated, Granny Hutch shot the shoat. They hitched Old Bess to the single tree which they had fitted between the shoat's hind feet. It was easier to drag the shoat to the washpot and swing him from a postoak limb than it was to carry boiling water to the shoat.

Finally, when they were through with Old Bess, Granny Hutch unharnessed her. Eve watched her and Tansy wander off along Dog Branch. I wish I could go with them, she thought. We would have such fun. But she kept on scraping the shoat's dirty, smelly hair. Eve meant to earn her keep.

She worked quietly all afternoon, Night caught them still cutting up hams and shoulders by lamplight. Neither wanted a bite of supper. Midnight came while they ground sausage. Next they stuffed them inside the cleaned intestines. When they had finished, they fell into their beds. For once, they left the washing up till morning.

"We'll render lard tomorrow," Granny Hutch said to Eve across the darkness. Neither of them could sleep. "And after we're through," she went on, "I'll make you some crackling bread. If you've never tasted crackling bread then you're in for a real treat. Only it's mighty rich. You eat too much, it can make you sick."

"What's a blue norther?" Eve asked. "I've always heard of them."

"Notice how still it is," Granny Hutch answered, rubbing her tired legs. "That's the way it gets before a blue Texas norther. Not a leaf moves. Everything just seems to stand out by itself."

Eve yawned. "Sounds like the prelude to a song," she said.

"Well now, I don't rightly know what that word *prelude* means. As for the song, I think it's ready to be sung. Listen."

A wind, high and keening, whistled out of the north. When it died away, Eve said, "That's funny. The stillness is back again."

Suddenly a wild burst of wind swooped down about the cabin. It flapped the loose boards on the smokehouse. "Here it is," Granny Hutch said. "It hit us just before day. And we haven't slept as it is."

Eve hopped out of bed. She lit the lamp and built a fire in the fireplace. In the fast chilling early dawn the remains of yesterday's hog killing looked grim and discouraging. She sighed as she looked at the messy table. "I do believe," she said to Granny Hutch, "that dirty dishes multiply."

They ate their breakfast grits and cleaned the kitchen. By now the washpan water Eve had dashed through the door was freezing on the stoop. She couldn't believe it. She had to go out and rub her finger across the rock. "Why," she said, "when we went to bed it was summer. I couldn't even bear to have the bed sheet over me." She grinned at Granny Hutch buttoning her high-topped shoes by the fire. "When we start to the lot," she said, "I'll need that sheet now to wrap up in."

Suddenly she sobered. "Tansy," she cried. "Will Tansy freeze?"

Granny Hutch brought Eve a long shawl. "Tansy's all right," she said. "Horses can stand a heap of cold. Horses and dogs."

The rooster and his hens were still crouched high on a limb of the big mesquite behind the corncrib. No amount of grain could coax them down. "Silly old things," Granny Hutch grumbled. "Weather like this they need every bite they can get."

"What's the matter with them?" Eve wanted to know. "Don't they know it's morning?"

"They're afraid," Granny Hutch told her. "They feel safer up on their roost."

Eve laughed. She watched the wind blow their tails. "Seems to me," she said, "they'd feel safer squatted on the ground."

They gave the calf half the milk. Then they put out extra water in the barrel for Old Rose. Already a skim of ice was forming where the cow had finished drinking. It was good finally to be back inside the warm cabin. It was good to sit by the fire and listen to the chimney draw.

They ate an early noon meal. The grits, hot from the iron pot, tasted fine with sugar and cream stirred in. Granny Hutch roasted one of the sausages. "Figure that will be one less sausage to hang and smoke," she said.

Eve tucked away plenty of food. She was reaching for a third helping of sausage when she thought of Tansy out there in the freezing winds. "You can stop your worry," Granny Hutch told her. "Old Bess will look after that colt. Likely as not, she'll take her to a thicket of liveoaks to keep off the wind."

"Couldn't I bring him here by the fire, Granny Hutch?"

Granny Hutch looked shocked. She said, "It's fine for folks to love animals. It's fine, too, for animals to love folks . But somewhere the Lord drew a line between them. Say you raised up Tansy like a human. When he had to go back to being an animal he wouldn't know how to take care of himself."

Eve said slowly, "I guess you're right. He'd be in a spot."

"Yes," Granny Hutch answered. "You let animals be animals, and folks be folks. Don't go about mixing them up."

Eve drank her milk. "Wonder if the chickens are down?"

"Can't say."

"And Old Rose. Wonder if her water is frozen?"

"Could be. We might have to turn her out where

she can water at Dog Branch."

"I guess the calf's all right. He's full of good, rich milk."

"Could be."

"And the shoat—" Eve jumped. She looked down at the sausage on her plate. "Excuse me, Granny Hutch," she said, "I've finished eating."

12

November slid by until it was Thanksgiving. Granny Hutch had never made any to-do over Thanksgiving. But Eve was a great one for observing special days. By Monday of that week she was planning the dinner. "We'll have sausage instead of turkey," she said. "And baked sweet potatoes and a loaf of fresh lightbread. Could we have some of those little peaches we dried, Granny Hutch, or maybe you could make them into a fruit cobbler."

"I could. But if I took a jar of canned peaches and made the cobbler it would be better." Granny Hutch thought a moment. "I could strip the top with a lattice of pie dough. Then I'd warm some butter and crumble brown sugar in it for a topping. Served hot with Old Rose's cream, it would be mighty fine."

Eve said, "Now we've got to figure out what we'll feed the animals." They were eating supper. She pushed her plate away to give room for thinking. "Old Bess and Tansy could have an extra armful of cane stalks. I'll shell a bit more corn for the chickens and for the—" She gave Granny Hutch a crooked smile. "I keep forgetting about the shoat," she said.

Still, Eve was disappointed because they didn't have a turkey for Thanksgiving.

"I've been hearing wild turkey toms gobbling early in the morning," Granny Hutch said. "Could be, I might get one."

"Oh, that would be perfect. Then all we'd need would be guests for Thanksgiving dinner."

"Well," Granny Hutch said, "we could ask John and Viry Devvies. Only Viry wouldn't come."

"No," said Eve, "Viry wouldn't come." Fun sparkled in her eyes. "And if she did come, she wouldn't eat with poor white trash."

Tuesday went by. Wednesday. Still they hadn't heard a peep out of the gobblers. Maybe they'd changed roosting places. Eve was disappointed, but they went right on with their fixings for Thanksgiving. They set the yeast that night for early bread baking on Thursday morning. They scrubbed yellow yams and cut down a sausage link. By then Granny Hutch declared that she was dead tired. "Eve," she grumbled, "I don't have that built-in excitement that keeps you going."

Eve, too, had been busy. Wednesday was a nice and sunny day for late November. She had scrubbed both floors. She'd polished the lamp globe until Granny Hutch declared she couldn't even see a globe on the lamp. They'd piled special wood against the chimney back. "Now," Eve said as they went to bed, "we've got everything but the turkey."

In her dreams the liveoaks on the other side of Dog

Branch were black with turkey gobblers. They were big toms with stiff beards that stood out from their breasts like goatees on old men. And the gobbling! One bunch would tune up. Then another bunch would come in. Never in her life had Eve heard such a racket.

"Eve. Eve." It was Granny Hutch shaking her. "The turkey toms. Do you hear them gobbling? Here, slip on your shoes while I wrap a coat about you. Can you see how to load the gun, or will I have to light the lamp?"

It wasn't quite daylight when they went through the front yard gate. Sure enough, the gobbling was down on Dog Branch, in the direction of the liveoaks. They hurried on. A shaft of light broke through the eastern sky. Now they could see the big toms bulking the oaks. They were getting ready to fly out and making enough noise, Eve thought, to be heard clear to Marty.

Granny Hutch motioned Eve back. She crept up as close as she dared to the trees. There was nothing now between Granny Hutch and the toms but a narrow strip of Dog Branch. She waited for more light. Two toms flew out of the trees. Eve watched them soar across Dog Branch. Her heart was in her throat.

Granny Hutch drew a bead on the blackest and thickest bulk and fired. There was a violent explosion. The gun kicked her left shoulder. Turkey toms whirred by. It seemed to Eve there must be hundreds of them.

They were gone. Eve was sick with disappointment. And then a tom came tumbling through the branches, striking the ground under the trees with a loud thud. Granny Hutch felt Eve's restraining hand. "You wait," she said, "I'll get him."

The tom was a beauty. Granny Hutch had shot him through the neck. "Now that's what I call good shooting," Eve said as they sat down to pick him.

"Shoo now," Granny Hutch said, "nothing but pure luck."

"Luck or not," Eve said happily, "we've got a turkey for Thanksgiving. And the wings will make a fine duster."

There was plenty of corn pone left over from the day before to make the stuffing. There'd be wild onions in it and what eggs Granny Hutch could spare. There was sage left over from making the sausage. And there was plenty of Old Rose's butter.

Eve wouldn't think of eating until she'd fixed dinner for the animals. Then she had to lead Tansy to the front yard gate to show Granny Hutch how well he led. And she had to show his latest trick, nibbling corn from her hand. "See how he leads," she said. "But then, I guess he knows he can't get away."

Granny Hutch smiled as she looked at the frayed piece of rope Eve had tied around Tansy's neck. "One little jerk," she said, "just one little pull, and that tattered rope would be in two."

But Eve knew that Tansy didn't want loose. Eve was Tansy's world. He would gladly have followed her all day. "Eve," Granny Hutch said, "it isn't given to many humans to have the touch with animals that you have."

"Couldn't I just sit on his back a teeny weeny

minute?" Eve begged. "I'd sit oh so easy."

"And have him swaybacked?"

"Well, I'll just have to wait till he's old enough."

And then she remembered. By the time Tansy was old enough to ride, she'd be back at the Home. Maybe something will keep turning up, she thought hopefully. I'll keep believing it will.

The white tablecloth was yellow from disuse, but they got it out of the wardrobe anyway. Eve brought in a brown crock of sumac leaves. She was lucky to find some that hadn't shed.

Granny Hutch got out her best china. Eve loved its Indian Tree design. She took out two linen napkins. She was carving the turkey when Eve came in from penning Tansy. She sniffed the good smells. The glory look was on her face now. "Oh," she said, "how lovely everything is. I'll get the yams out of the ashes. I can't wait. I'm as hungry as a mama wolf with seven pups."

"Eve," Granny Hutch gasped, "you never learned such talk as that at the Home."

Eve's eyes danced. She dried her face on the towel. "No," she said, "I heard Mr. Devvies say it."

"Well, you just look here," said Granny Hutch sternly, "the Home had made a lady out of you when you came here. I'm not sending you back using such talk. You hear?"

"Yes, Ma'am." Eve slid into her chair. She looked down at her plate so Granny Hutch couldn't see the fun in her eyes. They bowed their heads. Suddenly the mischief left Eve. "May I ask the blessing?" she said.

She was quiet for a moment. Then the words

came: "Thank you, God, for an honest-to-goodness Thanksgiving. Help the children back at the Home someday to have the kind of Thanksgiving I'm having today. This is the first, real Thanksgiving I've ever had in my life.

13

On Christmas Eve Granny Hutch said without thinking, "My lands, it's already Christmas!"

Eve began making plans. "We could do up the work," she said, "then we could drive to Marty for a few things and come right back. We ought to get back before night."

Granny Hutch had to tell her. "Eve," she said, "I'm most out of money. I won't have any more till I sell the calf. I hate to tell you this. But we can't buy things for Christmas. Besides, if I had enough money for Christmas I'd have to use it to send you back."

Eve's eyes widened. At the Home there had always been Christmas. "It's all right about me," she said. "But there are the animals. They have to have Christmas. You know how animals feel about it. They always kneel at midnight on Christmas Eve."

She thought a while as she ate her breakfast. At last she said, "I've figured it all out. You know that fold of red paper Mrs. Lambeck gave me from her store. The one the mice gnawed. Well, I'll make bells out of it. I'll tie bells around every animal's neck. Every animal on the place. Old Rose and her calf. Old

Bess and Tansy. Then I'll make an extra bell for Tansy's tail." She smiled at the idea. "I do hope," she said, "there'll be enough left to make a pretty red bow for your hair. Why, we don't need a thing from Marty. We got Christmas right here."

By now even Granny Hutch had caught the spirit. "I reckon I could make a cake," she said. "I've plenty of pecans and peaches. Why, it would be a right good tasting cake if I threw in a cupful of molasses."

"And we'll make popcorn balls to put in our stockings," Eve cried. "And one each for the animals. Oh, it's going to be such a fine Christmas."

Suddenly Eve thought of something. She got up to pour Granny Hutch more coffee. When she took the coffee pot back to the hearth she went on into the bedroom. She took the parcel John Devvies had tied on the bluethorn at the bend of the road. She was glad that Granny Hutch had made her bed that morning as soon as she got up. She wouldn't be finding the parcel until night. She gave the pillow a last pat and skipped back into the kitchen.

Christmas Eve was bright and clear. Eve was disappointed. "There ought to be snow," she said.

"Don't start pining now for snow," Granny Hutch warned. "Like as not, you'll see plenty of it before January's done."

Right after breakfast Eve tied the bells on the animals. She led Tansy past the window. "Look," she called to Granny Hutch, "doesn't Tansy look lovely?"

Granny Hutch opened the window a bit. She called out, "I declare you've got that colt to thinking he's people. Lead him back to the horse lot and come help me with the dishes."

Granny Hutch found her present when she went in to make her bed. She opened the wrapping and lifted out a white shawl. It was hand crocheted with pink roses embroidered about the edges. "Oh," she gasped in surprise, "it's lovely."

Eve's face shone. Never had she heard Granny Hutch exclaim before over anything pretty. She loves beauty, same as I do, Eve thought. Only I'm not ashamed to show it.

By now, though, Granny Hutch had become practical again. "Eve," she said, "what did that shawl cost?"

"The dollar Mr. Millican gave me. Do you think it's worth a dollar?"

Granny Hutch said slowly, "That shawl cost more than a dollar. It's handmade, and it's fitted to the shoulders. I see John Devvies has added some cash money to pay for it. He slipped up on my blind side the way you did. Now I don't have a thing to give you two."

"Oh, but you have, " Eve said dancing about the table. "You're our present. And you can't do a thing about it."

She stopped and sniffed. "That cake sure is smelling good," she said.

The cake wasn't done by noon. Neither were the popcorn balls. They had Christmas Eve dinner just as the sun slid behind the hills. Eve had found two candles stowed away in the smokehouse. They made the table look festive. Granny Hutch bowed her head to say the blessing. "Let me," cried Eve. "I stayed awake last night till I thought up a rhyme." She bowed her head and began:

"Listen to me, God, and hear me say
Thank you so much for Christ's birthday.
Bless Rose and her calf. Bless Tansy and Bess.
But it's Granny Hutch I most want you to bless."

"Eve," said Granny Hutch, "you didn't ask anything for yourself."

Eve was shocked. "But I've got everything. I've got you and Old Bess and Tansy and Old Rose and her calf. I've even got Mr. Devvies. When you've got it all, you don't need anything else." She thought a moment. Then she giggled. "I don't have Viry yet," she said.

They sat by the fire late that night. Eve read the Christmas story from Luke:

"And she brought forth her firstborn son, and wrapped him in swaddling clothes, and laid him in a manger; because there was no room for them in the inn. . . ."

Outside, the night was black and crowded with stars. The big mantel clock struck ten. Eve said, "We ought to go to bed now. If I'm not too sleepy I might want to get up when the clock strikes twelve. I might want to go out and see Tansy kneel."

Midnight came. Eve slept on. She'd had a busy day. The moon came up. It silvered the top of the tin roof over the smokehouse. The clock stopped striking twelve times. Eve woke. A stillness of such beauty lay all about her that she held her breath. "Silent Night, Holy Night," she and Granny Hutch had sung by the fire. Eve turned over to go back to sleep. Maybe out there in the horse lot Tansy was still kneeling . . .

The wintry sunshine held on for a week. Then a drizzling rain set in. It was hard for Eve and Granny Hutch to keep dry. There were so many outside chores to do. "At least," Eve said cheerfully as they shucked corn, "we don't have to carry any water. At the cabin we just have to set out buckets and pans under the leak of the roof. And all the animals have to do is look up and open their mouths."

"Well, I wish it would stop," Granny Hutch grumbled. "I know we need moisture. Still, I do wish the sun would come out long enough to dry a clothesline of wash. Besides, my bones are beginning to ache."

Eve laughed. "I think the sun is mildewed," she said.

That night a cold norther moved in.

The next morning Eve woke up before it was light. She snuggled down in her blanket and listened to the wind whip the raindrops against the windowpane. She thought it really slapped them hard. Well, she thought, maybe there'll be plenty of moisture in the spring.

Spring. Where would she be by spring? She knew that she was staying on borrowed time. "God," she whispered under the coverlet, "Are you awake? I need to talk to you."

She waited until she thought God was ready. Then she went on. "God, have you noticed Tansy lately?

He's a regular beauty. He has a little black shading on his legs now. Especially on his hind legs. And the star in his forehead really shows. I can't wait till he sheds in the spring. His winter coat makes him a bit shaggy.

"Now that's what I need to talk about. If you don't come up with some idea right away, Granny Hutch is going to cut out my dress. Then she's going to count out her eggs she has salted away in the big stone jar. If she figures up enough money she's going to crank the pickup some pretty day and haul me to Marty to take the bus. She simply can't get education out of her head. Now I know the Home was giving me a fine education. But what I can't make Granny Hutch see is that education is all about me, like the air. She thinks it just comes out of books. And besides, next term I could ride the school bus to Marty."

Light crept into the room. It lay across Granny Hutch's sleeping face. Eve was glad they'd stacked the wood high on either side of the fireplace before they went to bed. They'd stored the buckets and pans of water under the kitchen table. If it weren't for the livestock she and Granny Hutch could stay in bed till noon, if they wanted to.

Granny Hutch opened her eyes. "I thought I heard you whispering," she said to Eve.

"I was. I was having a little talk with God."

Granny Hutch opened her eyes wider. "You mean you were saying your prayers."

"No. I was just talking with God. Somehow, He and I get closer when we talk than when I say my prayers. When I pray I always feel that God's away up there, sitting on his throne. But when I tell Him I want to talk, He just seems to come right down by my side."

"Well," said Granny Hutch, "you do have the funniest ideas. I reckon, though, they're all right."

Suddenly she noticed how late it was. "Why," she cried, "I've stayed in this bed till after daylight. My lands, if Viry Devvies knew it, she'd tell it all over Marty."

She threw back the covers.

"No, you don't get up," Eve told her. "I'm building the fire this morning."

While Eve fanned the fire, she heard a funny, groaning sound. It came from the postoak. If I didn't know better, she thought, I'd just know that postoak was groaning. She looked around at the cold, gray-looking kitchen. Trees don't groan, she reminded herself.

The sound came again. "Eve, what's that funny, rubbing sound?" Granny Hutch called from the bedroom. "Do you hear it?"

Eve went to the kitchen window. Why, the postoak tree was groaning! Its limbs were covered with an inch of ice. The wind was rubbing them together. Some were popping off. The stake-and-rider fence was a solid coat of ice. The tumbled-down rock fence. Every bush and blade of grass between the cabin and Dog Branch.

The liveoaks along Dog Branch were in the worst trouble because they still had their leaves. "Granny Hutch," Eve cried, "look outside!"

Eve bounced about helping Granny Hutch dress. Her flannel gown slapped against her ankles as she ran back to the window. "Oh," she breathed, "it's beautiful. It's simply beautiful."

Granny Hutch said right behind her, "I could call it beautiful if I didn't have to think about the livestock. They won't be able to get a bite to eat except what we feed them. Then I'm worried about the timber. Of course, the postoaks and hackberries and the blackjacks don't have their leaves. Even the pecan trees along Dog Branch have all shed, but they can't stand much more ice. Now I'm really bothered about the liveoaks. I'd hate for them to break down. Liveoaks furnish green leaves for livestock in the winter."

Now Eve looked worried. "If Old Bess doesn't get plenty to eat," she said, "Tansy won't have enough milk."

They hurried with breakfast. Then they crept to the lot, for the ground was glassy. They went to the henhouse first. The chickens had stopped roosting in the big mesquite when the weather turned cold.

Eve strewed the corn on the henhouse floor. But the chickens just sat on their roosts and cackled. Eve was puzzled. "What's wrong with them?" She wanted to know. "They acted that way last November when we had the blizzard."

"They still think it's night," Granny Hutch told her. "A hen or a rooster don't judge their days by the clock."

Eve thought that was funny. She was still laughing when they started back to the cabin.

That was when Granny Hutch stepped in the hole. It was all iced over until she couldn't see it. The ice crust broke under her weight. Her left foot went through, twisting painfully as it wedged into the hole. The bucket of milk hit hard when she fell. Milk spread all over the ice then turned to ice itself. "Drat that gopher hole," Granny Hutch cried. "My ankle feels like a vise is twisting it."

Eve came running and sliding. It took both of them and a stout mesquite limb to get Granny Hutch to the cabin. Eve unbuttoned her high-topped shoes. Granny Hutch looked down at her swollen ankle. "I'm sick now two ways," she said. "I'm sick from pain. But most of all I'm sick from worry. Child, how in the world will you manage till I can walk again?"

Eve patted her arm. She set the iron kettle back on the coals. "Don't you worry, " she told Granny Hutch. "I'll get along fine. Just fine."

Granny Hutch was thankful for the supply of Epsom salt she had bought in the fall, the last time she and Eve had gone to Marty. "Finest medicine in the world for sprains," she said, as Eve put some in the wash pan of hot water.

All that day Granny Hutch sat with her foot in the hot salt solution. And every time Eve got a minute from the work, she reheated it.

Night came on. There was no let up to the ice. Likewise, there was no let up to the pain in Granny Hutch's ankle. Outside, the creakings and groanings came more often.

It was during the miserable days which followed that Eve found the sampler. Mrs. Lambeck had given it to Granny Hutch. But she'd never embroidered it.

Finished, the sampler would have a garland of pink roses framing the motto "God Bless Our Home." Eve had found it tucked under the doily on the lamp stand. "I'll cross stitch it for you," she told Granny Hutch, "while the weather's too bad for me to run with Tansy. I'll hang it over your bed when I've finished with it. Then when I go back to the Home you can look at it and think of me."

Granny Hutch was a long time answering. Presently she said, "You're making your stitches too long. Better rip them out."

Eve sighed as she pulled out the threads. The look she gave Granny Hutch carried a speck of mischief. "I hope," she said, "that when I get to heaven I won't have to be a sewing angel."

It was during the next week after the ice melted that it snowed. It was not the kind of wet, straggly snow that usually fell in the Hill Country. It was a foot-deep, flaky dry snow. It covered everything like a smooth white blanket. And everytime Eve caught up with all the work, she'd go outside and make a big mound of soft snowballs. These she threw at the animals.

"Tansy sure nickers when I chunk him," she told Granny Hutch. She had stamped into the kitchen to lay a stump on the fire.

"Eve," Granny Hutch said as she bent over to lay it on, "you fair take away my breath. That stump is bigger than you. I just wanted to hold your dress tail I was that afraid you might topple over into the fire."

Granny Hutch complained miserably because Eve

had to work so hard. She said, "I'll be mighty glad when I can shoulder my share of the work again. And wait on me, too."

"Fiddle, " Eve scoffed, "I don't mind it. I just make believe I'm your grandchild." She looked at Granny Hutch. There was a hint of begging in her eyes. "It's no wrong," she said, "if I want to make believe I'm your grandchild." She came over to Granny Hutch. She touched her ever so lightly on the shoulder. "It's fun," she said, "playing you're my granny."

Granny Hutch moved her crippled ankle impatiently. "That," she said, "doesn't help my feelings one bit."

The day the thaw began, Granny Hutch was able to crow–hop with the help of the mesquite limb. Eve grieved because she didn't have a crutch. "I could ride over and borrow the one you said John Devvies has."

"You let John Devvies know I'm laid up and he'll be over here every day."

"Fine," Eve said. "Besides, Mr. Devvies is good company."

"Yes, and Viry'll give him fits. Next thing, he'll be tearing out to Marty. Now the weather isn't fitting for a trip to Marty. He might get bad crippled."

Eve finished setting the table. Then she came over to help Granny Hutch to her chair. "You really like to keep that big wall of pride around you," she said. She slid the mound of cornbread from the Dutch oven. Granny Hutch bowed her head for the blessing.

The following day the thaw was running little rivers between the cabin and Dog Branch. Eve thought of something. She ran to the almanac. "Why," she said wonderingly, "it's my birthday. The Home figured January 19, as the best date to set when I came."

Granny Hutch sat lost in thought before the fire. Presently she said, "Before you go out to the lot I wish you would count the eggs in the milk cooler."

"There's not but five," Eve counted, "The hens haven't laid much during this spell. Guess they figured we wouldn't want them to lay frozen eggs."

"Five eggs, " Granny Hutch mused. "Now count the matches."

"Count the matches." Eve went over to the tin match container. "Thirty-seven," she called out. "But don't worry. If they run out we can always light from the fire."

"Well, now go on to the lot. Don't be in too big a hurry to get back. I'll be all right."

Eve thought she heard Granny Hutch hobbling around when she came through the bedroom door. She must have been mistaken. Granny Hutch was right where she'd left her. In front of the fire.

The breakfast dishes on the table were covered with a clean dish towel. "Just leave them," Granny Hutch said sharply as Eve went over to the table. "You warm good. Then go out and take Old Bess and Tansy to Dog Branch for water. And you can stay out a bit with Tansy. Mind you, though, that you don't run. You'll wind up crippled like me."

Later Eve opened the bedroom door. She sniffed. "Something sure smells good," she said. The kitchen table had been cleared of its dishes. Now a hastily iced cake stood in its center. Thirteen matches burned on its top.

"Happy Birthday, Eve," Granny Hutch said.

Eve's eyes widened. She came slowly into the kitchen. She looked from the cake to Granny Hutch. Suddenly tears spilled down her cheeks. She ran back and shut the bedroom door with a bang. Then she ran to where Granny Hutch was sitting by the fire. She scooped her up in one big bear hug. She kissed her first on one wrinkled cheek and then the other. "Granny Hutch," she sobbed. "Oh, Granny Hutch!"

14

April came in, warm and yeasty. The winter hills colored up with pale green trees and masses of white plum blossoms. Here and there a sprinkling of redbud peeked through the scruboak. The corn was knee high and full of good growing. The whippoorwill peas had burst the ground crust, uncurling puny leaves and tender stalks.

"We'd better wash this morning," Granny Hutch said. "Tomorrow we'll be going up and down the corn middles with our hoes. The weeds are taking over. I saw a big tie vine we missed the other hoeing. Soon he'll dress up in purplish-red flowers and look so pretty you'll hate to cut him up. But pretty or not, he's got to come out if the corn has room to grow."

Eve jumped up from the table. She ran to the door to rid her lap of cornbread crumbs. "I'll build a fire around the washpot after I've filled it up," she said. She came back to the table where Granny Hutch was finishing her last cup of coffee. Eve's eyes were bright now with fun. "I love to go out to the washpot," she said. "I think it looks just like a fussy old black hen standing up in her nest. You almost expect her to look under to see if she's laid."

Granny Hutch shook her head and smiled. "Eve, Eve," she said, "I never know what you'll think of next."

Eve got a bucket and skipped on out to fill the pot.

Suddenly she stopped skipping. She sniffed. Whatever in the world was that heavenly fragrance? Then she knew. It came from the neck of the field John Devvies had neglected to break. The neck of the field was solid now with yellow daisies. Eve left the washpot and went out among them. She knelt down to part their milky-veined leaves. "You're so sweet, " she murmured, burying her face in them. "You remind me of—of resurrections of gold." She ran back toward the kitchen window. "Granny Hutch," she called, "take your hands out of the dishwater and put your head out the window. Take a deep breath. You'll get a whiff of heaven."

Granny Hutch put her head out and sniffed. "Honey daisies," she said. "No wonder the bees like them."

"Miss Woodruff called them huisache daisies," Eve said.

"Well, the name doesn't make any never mind to the bees. All they're after is their nectar."

Eve went slowly back to the washpot. She watched the sun touch up the yellow color of the flowers. They had spread solidly over the jut of land, even to the rock fence. She had told Granny Hutch to put her head out the window for a whiff of heaven. Was heaven, then, near or far, depending on where you looked? She went on down to Dog Branch to fill her bucket.

She filled the washpot. Then she went back to the cabin for coals. She saw how the postoak by the kitchen window had leafed out with big tender leaves. She thought she could see the first faint beginning of an acorn crop. I've surely been blind the past week, she thought. Now all those daisies didn't suddenly bloom out this morning. And that postoak didn't uncurl its leaves just now. She dragged up some wood. It was just too bad that folks' eyes really saw just now and then.

The next Sunday was Easter. The morning was the kind Eve said all Easter Sundays ought to be. The sky was clear. The sun had a golden touch. From the clumps of shinoak along the far side of Dog Branch she heard the redbirds sound their clear "Sweet-Sweet." The mockingbirds answered with their fluted warble, like water running down Dog Branch. She said to Granny Hutch, "I'm going to make Easter baskets."

"Well," Granny Hutch was counting hard. "I can spare six eggs, I reckon. That would be four for your nest and two for mine. But what will you use to make the baskets?"

"I'll use china bowls and line them with blue-bonnets." She came over to where Granny Hutch was taking eggs out of the milk cooler. "I'll need three china bowls," she said. "But I won't need any eggs for the third bowl, just bluebonnets."

Granny Hutch said, "I reckon the third bowl's for Tansy."

"No," Eve answered. "The third bowl's for Cindy's grave."

Granny Hutch turned her back quickly. She was a long time answering. Finally she said, "Get the bowls and make the baskets. I'll color the eggs."

"But we don't have any dye."

"I'll color them," Granny Hutch told her. "It's my secret."

"Oh, then, I'll stay and share your secret," Eve said. "I can decorate the bowls later."

Granny Hutch brought a flour sack of cloth scraps, and Eve helped her go through them. There was a scrap of bunting from John Devvies' lemonade stand. Granny Hutch turned the scrap until she found the stars. Then she snipped off the scrap and sewed it around an egg. Eve fished out a bit of red-flowered print. Granny Hutch sewed it around the second egg. There was a scrap of pink cloth with blue forget-me-nots. Then Granny Hutch found a piece of window curtain material with a small yellow tulip.

It was fun to Eve. "It's almost like hunting Easter eggs," she said happily. "Now we just need one more." Suddenly she said, "Oh, Granny Hutch, snip off just a corner of the print you have to make me a new dress."

Granny Hutch's face closed tightly. "We'll be making that dress right away," she said. "I can use my crippled foot now to treadle the machine. Just leave that cloth alone till we get ready to cut into it."

Now why did I have to bring that up, Eve thought sadly.

After Granny Hutch finished boiling the cloth--

covered eggs, she dropped them into cool water. Sometime later she unwrapped them. They were lovely. Eve couldn't help but be happy over them. She went out to fill the bowls with wildflowers.

She came back presently with two baskets interwoven with bluebonnets and sweet-smelling yarrow. "I even found some Sweet Williams," she said. "Just a few. I'm afraid that Old Rose grazes them." She came close to Granny Hutch. "I filled Cindy's bowl with water first," she said. "Then I put in the flowers. It looked pretty on her grave."

Granny Hutch said, "When the day is over, pick out two eggs you want to keep for a while. If the dye hasn't gone through the shell we'll have to eat the other four. After you're tired of the two, you can crumble them to the chickens. Can't afford to waste them, you know."

"I'll keep the one with the stars," Eve said happily. "And I'll keep the white one with the red rose."

For Easter dinner Granny Hutch said they could splurge a bit. They cut off some choice slices of ham. There were plenty of tender lambs quarter greens growing in the flats along Dog Branch. Granny Hutch opened a jar of her scanty supply of peaches. "Maybe there'll be plenty of seedling peaches this year," she said hopefully.

After they'd eaten, Eve set the two Easter baskets in the kitchen window. Then she went to the wardrobe. She took down Mr. Hutch's Bible and began reading in a high, clear voice from the thirteenth chapter of Acts:

"And when they had fulfilled all that was written of him, they took him down from the tree, and laid him in a sepulchre. But God raised him from the dead: And he was seen many days of them which came up with him from Galilee to Jerusalem, who are his witnesses unto the people. And we declare unto you glad tidings how that the promise which was made unto the fathers.

God hath fulfilled the same unto us, their children, in that he hath raised up Jesus again; as it is also written in the second psalm, thou art my son, this day have I begotten thee."

A wind, tender and filled with the scent of wildflowers, came through the kitchen door. Eve put away the Bible. "It's been a good Easter Sunday," she said.

That night Old Bess and Tansy didn't come out of the calf pasture for their nightly feed of corn nubbins.

15

Eve and Granny Hutch found them the next afternoon, where they stood in the thickest tangle of the bee myrtle. Old Bess saw them and whinnied pitifully. Eve felt a fear like a cold hand clutching her heart. She pushed through the scratching, sweet-smelling bush until she saw them.

Tansy stood beside Old Bess. His head was down almost to the ground and his left front leg was swollen the size of a butter churn. When Eve cried out, Granny Hutch pushed through the twisted, stickery brush as if it weren't there. "Eve," she gasped, "don't move till I get there. Do you hear me? Don't move." She went up to the colt and lifted his leg. There it was, plain to see: two fang marks, wide apart and little bigger than hatpin points. "It's Mr. Captain," she told Eve. "He must have bitten Tansy sometime yesterday."

"Why didn't you leave your work and help me hunt for Tansy?" Eve cried wildly. "I begged you to go. You wouldn't even let me go. We might have saved him."

Granny Hutch looked at the sun. It was sliding

toward the western hills. "Eve," she said, "we can't save Tansy now. The poison has done its work."

It was as if an evil hand had passed over Eve's face, leaving it old now and filled with hate. "I'll kill Mr. Captain," she screamed. "I'll kill him with my bare hands." And there in the red dirt where Tansy had pawed out his misery, Eve flung herself down. She fell face first. Her fingers clawed and squeezed the grass roots as if they were Mr. Captain.

Granny Hutch tried to lift her, but Eve twisted out of her hands. "Leave me alone," she begged. Her voice was high-pitched with bitterness. "Just go away and leave me alone."

Granny Hutch tried getting Tansy to walk. But it was no use. Finally the colt lay down beside Eve. Eve flung an arm about his neck and pulled his head against hers. "Eve," Granny Hutch said, "I'm going back for liniment and bandages. Whatever you do, don't move till I get back with the lantern. Likely as not, Mr. Captain is still around."

Eve did not answer.

Bees were droning from one sweet-scented clump of myrtle to another by the time Granny Hutch got back. She carried with her a lantern, liniment, and a bucket of fresh water for Tansy to drink.

But it was too late. Tansy was dead.

Dark settled down, heavy and threatening. Still Eve lay there, Tansy's head against her own. "Eve," Granny Hutch tried again, "Mr. Captain may be coiled right near where we are standing. Or else his mate may be around. Generally where you find one rattlesnake, you find the other."

No answer. Eve still lay crumpled as if a hand had twisted her.

A star came out, and then another. The moon would be late. Granny Hutch tried sternness. She shook Eve by the shoulder. Eve twisted away. Finally Granny Hutch said, "Eve, I've worked hard today. I'm old, and I'm tired. If Mr. Captain bites me here I'd never make it to the cabin. Then what would you do? You'd be left here by yourself. Please. I'm afraid of Mr. Captain."

Without a word Eve got up.

When they had gone inside the house and lit the lamp Granny Hutch said, "I wish you could just forget tonight. But that kind of a curtain wasn't handed us. The only curtain we have is one that shuts off to-morrow."

Midnight came. Still they sat. The moon showed up, swelling brightly from the tree line. Granny Hutch said, "Would you like to go out and sit on the stoop?"

"Could we?" A hint of eagerness showed in Eve's voice. How long they sat outside neither knew. The moon sailed over the cabin and headed westward. A mockingbird tuned up with such a jumble of joy in the postoak that Eve bounced off the stoop. She ran to the corner of the cabin and threw a stick in the direction of the tree. "Scat, you," she hissed. Whether the bird flew or not she never knew. Anyway, it hushed.

They buried Tansy the next day up in the neck of the far field where he had been born. Only the tansy asters didn't purple the postoak woodland now. The death's camass grew where water from the last rain stood. Granny Hutch told Eve it was so named because its black, coated bulb carried death to anything that mouthed it. Where they dug, it lifted round-topped clusters of innocent-looking, cream-colored flowers.

It was late afternoon when they started back to the cabin. All about them wildflowers bloomed, and their mixed perfumes were heady and sweet. Bluebonnets stretched to the far side of the gravelly wash. Perfume balls nodded from the banks of the stock pond. The buttercup family bloomed across the long-plowed but unplanted land. There was the yellow evening primrose with its four petals that last only a day. The flutter mill clung to the sides of the furrows. Even the little honeysuckle primrose had opened its pink and white blooms like a fan by the time they left the field.

Eve had said scarcely a word since coming to the cabin the night before. She had eaten nothing. Granny Hutch looked worried. They went to bed early. As Eve undressed, Granny Hutch said to her, "Eve, would you like to sleep in the big bed with me?"

16

The old dominecker hen stepped out of the tall weeds behind the cowlot. She had eight biddies. Each biddy had a black stripe up and down its back. Eve helped Granny Hutch drive them to a coop. A flicker of life showed in her face.

She didn't traipse up and down Dog Branch with Old Bess now. She stayed close to Granny Hutch. When she had been happy, sometimes in her enjoyment she forgot her chores. Now she remembered them all. "It grieves me," Granny Hutch told her. "You're not a little girl any more. You're a sober woman now in a little girl's body."

And then it was May. There had been enough rain to give the fields and woodland color. The June bugs began to sound off even if it weren't June. They made such a sharp rattling Granny Hutch declared the sound made her jump clean out of her hide. She and Eve hoed the weeds out of the watermelon vines. Eve was careful now to lift each fast-growing vine with her hoe.

Tarantulas walked high on their black furry legs. They would stop whenever they saw Eve and Granny

Hutch and would point their longest leg at them like a finger. Granny Hutch told Eve they weren't as harmful as folks said they were. She warned her, though, that an angry tarantula could jump as high as a man's head.

Eve hoed carefully around one. "I'll try not to make him lose his temper," she said. The tiniest smile worked at the corners of her mouth. "I don't want him jumping up to look me in the eye."

Old Bess stumbled out of the woodland and through the melon vines. She made such a mess they had to drive her away. Old Bess was lonesome too.

"As soon as we get the hoeing done," Eve said, "I'm ready to go back to the Home."

"But I can't send you back till you pick up a bit," Granny Hutch worried. "Since we lost Tansy you haven't eaten as much as a bird. If I send you back looking like this the Home will think I beat you and starved you." She leaned on her hoe and studied Eve. "Do you want to go back now?" she asked.

Eve straightened out a melon vine. "No," she said, "I can't say that I want to go back. I just don't care anymore."

"Well, as soon as you mend a bit there's really nothing to keep us from driving to Marty and putting you on the bus. I have enough money now."

The next morning they heard John Devvies' pickup tearing over the hill. Eve watched him sitting straight, his legs braced wide apart. Then just as he turned toward the yard gate he let out his blood-curdling yell. Eve laughed. "He doesn't scare me any more with his Rebel yell," she said.

Granny Hutch shook her head. "Viry must really be after him this time," she told Eve.

John Devvies stamped through the kitchen door. The dogs were at his heels. But just as Liver Pill put out a forepaw to enter the door, John Devvies shut it. "He, he, he," John Devvies laughed. "Fooled you this time, Granny Hutch."

He caught Eve's chin and turned her face up to his. He studied her for a moment. "Yep," he said, "soon as I heard about Tansy I said, 'There goes the glory look.'"

"If you're going to Marty," Eve said, "I'll ride along with you. It will save Granny Hutch a trip. You see, I've decided to go back to the Home."

"Hold it, hold it," John Devvies boomed, "I'm not taking you anywhere till you put on that glory look again. Besides, I'm not headed for Marty. If I had been, I'd not have come by here. No siree. I come to make you and Granny Hutch a visit. And I come with some news I figured would make Glory Girl here smile again." He looked first at Granny Hutch and then at Eve. "Now get set," he said, "for I'm fixing to tell it." He let out a deep breath. "I figure Old Bess is in foal again."

"Oh," cried Eve, "I can't wait. I just can't wait. We could name the new colt 'Tansy Too.'" Then she remembered. "Only I won't be here," she said. "I finally told Granny Hutch she was right. I'm going back as soon as I get a way to the bus."

John Devvies looked crestfallen. "Run my old pickup all this way to see the glory look and before it got good spread it's gone." He glared at Eve. "So you're finally running out," he said. "Here I been laying off coming to see you and Granny Hutch all this time so I wouldn't have to haul you to Marty. Then you decide to go back yourself. Beats all." He stalked out the door and climbed into his truck. Slowly he turned around. From the pickup bed the hounds looked back at Eve so dejectedly she had to laugh.

"Well," said Granny Hutch, "there's dewberries up Dog Branch just wasting for want of picking. Since you won't be going today, we might as well go get a few."

Eve went out and got the buckets from the back yard fence.

They crossed upper Dog Branch. The watercress was blooming now and toughening. There'd be no more good meals of vinegar, brown sugar, and salt added to hot grease, then all of it poured over tender watercress and wild onions.

Eve walked ahead. Her thoughts were whirling around Tansy Too. Even if I won't be here, she thought, it's going to be mighty nice for Old Bess and Granny Hutch. Without realizing she began to hum, "Froggie Went A Courtin'." Thank you, God, she thought, it's a beginning.

Behind her she heard a stumbling. She stopped to wait for Old Bess.

They were a few days late, for the berries were getting overripe and dropping from the vines. But there still were plenty to pick. "If we get back in time," Granny Hutch promised, "I'll make you a berry cobbler."

Eve was eating as many berries as she dropped into her bucket. She said with her mouth full, "A pie would be good. But it couldn't be any better than the berries on the vine. It just couldn't be."

A cloud sailed under the sun. Then it floated away. Farther up Dog Branch they heard John Devvies' stallion whinny. Then he came on a run. He jumped the stake-and-rider fence and went off down Dog Branch with Old Bess. Granny Hutch took off her bonnet and fanned herself. "Well," she said, "Old Bess had one mighty fine colt. I figure maybe she can have another."

The next day Granny Hutch made the berry cobbler. She cooked the berries with brown sugar and a little water until they were bubbling in thin syrup. Then she made the crust. She covered the top with lattice-stripped dough and a mixture of butter, sugar, and cinnamon. Eve watched it all. Then she got the cedar water bucket and went down to Dog Branch to fill it.

When she came in again her bonnet was swinging against her back. Her hair, partly unplaited, was trying to curl. Color showed in her face. Granny Hutch looked pleased. "If John Devvies could see you," she said, "he'd declare that glory look was mighty close."

Eve wrinkled her nose. "The pie smells good," she said. "It's got a special smell, but I can't decide just what it smells like."

"Well," said Granny Hutch, "could be it just smells like berry pie."

They sat down and bowed their heads. "God,

please bless this food," Eve said. She never was one to chant a fixed blessing. She thought a moment, but the cobbler smell covered all her thoughts. "Amen," she said and dipped a big spoon into the thick red juice.

They kept the rest of the berries in the cooler. "If we'd been a week earlier," Granny Hutch said, "we'd have plenty of berries to can. There's a good crop of wild honey this year, so sweetening wouldn't have been a problem. John Devvies found a bee tree on the other side of the rock fence. He's got it marked with his big X. When he robs it, he'll see to it that we get plenty of the honey."

"But why would he mark it with a big X?" Eve wanted to know. Granny Hutch told her how a man crossing any other man's land could find a bee tree and it would be his. He would slash his own particular mark on that tree and nobody else would cut it. "It's like marking or branding cattle," Granny Hutch said.

That evening after supper Eve said, "Could we sit out on the stoop till bedtime? Maybe you could sing 'Froggie Went A Courtin'.'"

"I will," Granny Hutch promised her. "But only if you sing with me."

They sat down on the stoop. They listened for a while to Dog Branch gurgling over the smooth rocks. Eve's head was filled with dreams of Tansy Too. Even if I never see the colt, she thought, I can always think about it. Softly she began to sing,

> "Froggie went a courtin', he did ride,
> Latta-Bota-Rincktum-Kime-O . . ."

17

By now they could bring themselves to talk about Tansy. They even began hunting again for Mr. Captain. They covered every sandy wash looking for the zigzag track a rattlesnake makes by holding its rattles above the ground when it crawls. "You can figure the size of a snake," Granny Hutch told Eve, "by the width and crookedness of that track. If it's a big snake with a lot of rattles, it'll make a mighty wide and crooked track."

They felt sure that Mr. Captain was hidden in the rock fence. They were careful as they beat the weeds and grasses nearby.

"Maybe he's sorry about Tansy and has crawled away," Eve said.

"Land sakes, child, a rattlesnake doesn't feel shame for what it does. It just does what it's learned by nature. Or maybe by the devil. I'm sure I don't know which."

Eve stopped at a tall sunflower. She pushed it until it swayed, Finally its top bloom touched the ground. "Look," she said. Some of her former mischief showed again. "I've got this sunflower in a spot. I've made it turn its back to the sun." She let the sunflower go and said, "I wonder about rattlesnakes. I know that if we find Mr. Captain we'll have to kill him. We'll have to. We won't be safe with him around. Then, too, he could bite any of the animals. Still, I wonder why. I don't like to kill."

"It's a way of life, I reckon, " Granny Hutch told her, "Sometimes it's kill or be killed, But I don't know why. Seems like all the years I've lived ought to give me the answers. But it doesn't."

June came. Granny Hutch didn't say a word about sending Eve back. One night as they sat out on the stoop listening to the katydids, Eve mentioned it. "I don't really want to go back," she said. "But it's time."

The evening breeze was hot. Down along Dog Branch the fireflies flitted among the tall reeds like tiny falling stars. "I'll get you ready soon," Granny Hutch said.

"Don't send me back while you need me."

"Well, I thought that while you were here we'd pull some of the roasting ears. We'll cut off some of the kernels for drying. Now the whippoorwill peas look like they're making a bumper crop. We wouldn't want them to waste."

Eve let her breath go softly. It would be a while. Right now, she was needed. That was all she wanted to hear.

They found Mr. Captain the last week in June. They'd started early that morning picking peas before the dew dried on the pods. Canning peas was what Granny Hutch called uphill business, because peas have no acid. At the cabin they sealed the jars of cooked peas by melting sealing wax and spooning it around the lids.

Finally Granny Hutch lifted the last jar from the molasses bucket of boiling water. Eve was ready with the sealing wax. Then Granny Hutch wiped the perspiration from her face and said, "Let's go to the melon patch. I came on a striped one in the shade of a mesquite the other day when I was in the patch. Its curl was dead, and it was full of plunk. We'll take the butcher knife and a salt shaker with us and have a feast right there."

Eve skipped along beside her as they went to the melon patch. Granny Hutch said suddenly, "I hope before you go you get that glory look on your face again. I've been missing it."

"I'm getting it back," Eve told her. "Sometimes I get it a little whenever I think of Tansy Too. Even if I don't get to see Tansy Too you can write me."

At the melon patch Granny Hutch pulled the big striped melon. When she cut it the knife cleaved it neatly. It was that ripe. Granny Hutch smiled when she heard Eve exclaiming over the red heart. It was already getting its own coat of sugar before they could even take a bite. "Well," Granny Hutch said, "you don't exactly have the glory look, but you're coming mighty close."

Suddenly there was a dry, hollow rattle. It sounded to Eve like the scurrying of dead leaves. Only it was quicker, more threatening. Then a long, rusty-scaled snake hurtled its body toward Eve. Granny Hutch cried out, but Eve had already jumped backward. Her scream was all that Mr. Captain needed to make him coil again.

And they didn't even have a hoe.

The melon patch, though, was on a slope of ground. The swift spring rains had washed bunches of sand rock to the edge of the patch. Even, though, with plenty of rocks to throw, it was a long, hard battle. Mr. Captain fought every inch of the way. He coiled, rattled, then hurtled his big body toward whoever was closer to him. His flat-topped head was split by his angry mouth. His jaws were heavy with poison and his fangs were already throwing it.

Finally one of Granny Hutch's rocks broke his back. Eve knew that he couldn't strike now, because a rattlesnake has to make a steel spring of its body before it can jump. Both Eve and Granny Hutch had hit him many times. With his thick body coiled, though, the rocks had bounced off like hitting rubber.

When it was over they stood looking at Mr. Captain's crushed head and body. He was better than five feet long and bigger around than the upper part of a man's arm. Eve saw that Granny Hutch was so spent she scarcely could move. The air about them reeked with the scent of the snake's poison. It hung like a heavy mist in the air. Suddenly Eve sat down on the ground and was sick.

All through the battle sugar had kept beading the heart of the melon halves. But now, of course, they couldn't eat it. The fight had taken place right over the melon. Even the halves reeked with the sickening poison. Eve looked up at Granny Hutch. Granny Hutch sank down beside her. "I don't know why it had to be, Eve. I just feel, though, that you're going to keep hunting till you find the answers."

18

The days became a blur to Eve. She worked hard now for two reasons. She knew that Granny Hutch needed her help. Most of all, though, she worked hard so she could sleep at nights. She'd wake in the morning and lie on her cot drowsily for a moment. Something lay heavily on her mind, but she couldn't come awake enough to know what it was. Then she would know. And knowing made the days heavy indeed.

July came. Granny Hutch said to Eve, "John Devvies bought half a dozen of my oldest hens. He came yesterday while you and Old Bess traipsed up and down Dog Branch. He paid me for them. Now I really have enough money to send you back to the Home."

Eve's face whitened under her freckles. "I knew I was overstaying," she said.

"I'll start sewing your clothes. I don't aim to send you off with nothing but the clothes you have on your back."

She made Eve two dresses. One was the new print. It was such a pretty pattern, brown background all sprigged with little red posies. She made the neck high to hide Eve's spindly throat. The long sleeves covered her thin, brier-scratched arms. Then she ruffled both the neck and the wrists. "It will be a good dress for you to wear to school," she decided. "I'm right ashamed I've kept you out one whole term. You could have learned so much in that time."

"I did learn a lot," Eve said, trying on the dress. "I learned lessons I could never have learned in the classroom."

Granny Hutch smiled as she pinned up the hem. "Lessons like making Old Rose back her foot?" she asked.

"Yes," said Eve, "like making Old Rose back her foot."

Granny Hutch made Eve's other dress from her own wedding gown. It was of white cashmere. She had to cut carefully in order to find enough cloth the moths hadn't ruined. "It's so pretty," Eve told her. "I never had a white dress before."

"It will do for a while," Granny Hutch said.

She took down the bedroom curtain to make Eve a ruffled petticoat. "Oh, but you shouldn't," Eve protested.

But Granny Hutch went on cutting. "Come winter," she said, "I aim to get me some dark material so I can't see how cold it is outside."

Come winter. Eve looked at Granny Hutch and thought how old she looked. Could she make winter? Would Old Bess have Tansy Too by then? And would the wild turkey gobblers roost again in the liveoaks on Dog Branch?

By the middle of the week Granny Hutch had finished with the sewing. "It's the day before the Glorious Fourth," she told Eve. "I figure John and Viry Devvies will be driving by. He didn't put in for the lemonade stand this year. Still, I figure they'll go to Marty. We'll have you ready. Then I don't see how he can refuse to take you along."

Eve knew why Granny Hutch didn't go to the Marty Reunion. Her melons were late. And there weren't too many. Eve was glad they hadn't planned to go. Somehow, it brought back too many memories.

She said to Granny Hutch, "Why don't you let me send a letter to Mr. Cooley, the truant officer at the Home? He could come get me and you would have the bus money for winter. You'll need it."

"And have the Home vexed because they had to spend the money to get you? Eve, you've helped me a sight. I aim for you to ride that bus back like quality folks."

That afternoon Eve walked with Old Bess again. It was like it had been between them before Tansy came. They crossed Dog Branch and came out on the side of the liveoaks. A crow flew squawking out of the trees.

Eve watched it disappear among the pasture trees. She said to Old Bess, "I wish you could go back with me. But of course you can't. Then one of these days Tansy Too will come, and besides, you do have to stay and help Granny Hutch." She wound her arms around the mare's neck. "I do wish I could have seen Tansy Too before I went back," she said. "But I guess there's no end to things. Life just goes on and on and on. Like one big circle."

As they walked toward the cabin they talked about Tansy. For between Eve and the big stumbling mare there was a bond, that same bond there'd been between Eve and Tansy. "It's given to a few folks the gift of talking with animals," Granny Hutch had said often. "But it's given to a powerful few."

The minute Eve saw the car come around the road bend she knew it was the truant officer. She and Old Bess were almost at the horse lot. Eve shut the lot gate and hurried to the cabin. By coming in at the north bedroom door she was hidden from the man when he got out of the car.

Granny Hutch had come in from setting a hen in the corncrib. She had put some potatoes on to boil and had gone out to the mint bed on the east side of the cabin. Eve knew that Granny Hutch was picking mint leaves to spice the peach drink she had cooling in the kitchen window.

The man who came up the walk was thin and tired-looking. He carried a satchel and wore a black derby. He cleared his throat when he saw Granny Hutch with the mint leaves in her hands. "I'm Maurice Cooley," he said. "I'm a truant officer at Home of the Tyne." He pulled back his coat to show his badge.

Eve watched him worry with his derby. Then he cleared his throat again. "I'm looking for a girl about twelve years old. Her name is Eve Sheldon. She ran away from the Home several months ago. She wrote her teacher, Miss Woodruff, that she was in the Hill Country. She wouldn't say where, but it must be out away from any town. She said she was happy with the animals, so I figured it must be away from any large settlement."

Behind the open bedroom door Eve could see him and Granny Hutch, where they stood by the stoop. She could see the tender mint leaves growing limp in Granny Hutch's hands. She knew they couldn't see her, but she thought her heart would burst from its hard beating.

When Granny Hutch didn't answer, the man went on. "The children at the Home said that Eve always talked of running away to the Texas Hill Country. Now I've checked all the small settlements. In Miss Woodruff's letter Eve talked about living far from any town. But even checking the thinly settled country is a big job, I can tell you. Besides, I don't believe Hill folk tell what they do know." He stopped and searched Granny Hutch's face. Eve watched his black mustache quiver with eagerness. He said, "Could you by any chance have seen or heard of this girl?"

Why don't I just call out and say, I'm in the bedroom, Mr. Cooley? Why don't I go out and beg him to let me stay, Eve thought. It would be a lot easier on Granny Hutch. Besides, my things are packed, and Granny Hutch would have the bus money for winter. Why don't I? I just don't know why. But I can't. And I sure can't beg.

Still Granny Hutch hadn't said a word.

Outside, Eve could hear Old Bess nicker to be let out of the horse lot. It will be over soon as Granny Hutch answers, Eve thought.

The truant officer tried again. This time he spoke

sternly, "Could she by any chance be living in your cabin?"

Suddenly Granny Hutch spoke. Her words were blunt, but they were straight to the point. "No," she said, "I don't reckon there's anybody lives here but me and my grandchild."